PARENTHOOD
Without
*Hassles**

* well almost

Dr. Kevin Leman

Harvest House Publishers
Eugene, Oregon 97402

PARENTHOOD WITHOUT HASSLES, (WELL, ALMOST)

Copyright ©1979 Harvest House Publishers
Eugene, Oregon 97402
Library of Congress Catalog Card Number: 78-65621
ISBN # 0-89081-183-0 Trade
        0-89081-304-3 Mass

Printed in the United States of America.

WITH SPECIAL RECOGNITION

to

My High School Counselor

who told me, "Leman, with your disciplinary record and grades in this school, I couldn't get you into reform school."

IN LOVING MEMORY
of
THREE VERY SPECIAL PEOPLE
Will Wright
Clifford Loomis
and
six-year-old
JoAnn Kristine Holt

THANK YOU . . .

To the people I love—my parents, John and May Leman; my brother, Jack; my sister, Sally Chall; my godmother, Edna Wright; the three treasures of my life, daughters Holly and Kristin and son Kevin. Most of all, thank you to my loving wife and chief editorial assistant, Sande, whose comfort, encouragement, and love have provided me with the motivation necessary for such an undertaking.

Thank you to Vivian Stumpf for her valuable assistance in the preparation of the manuscript; to Bob Hawkins, president of Harvest House, for giving me an opportunity to share with others; to Dr. Oscar C. Christensen, my major professor, with whom I studied for five years, for influencing my professional life so greatly; to Eleanor Wilson, my high school geometry teacher, for her encouragement, insight, and wisdom; to Dr. Ken Olson for his much-needed counsel and encouragement; to Adolfo Quezada for his timely suggestions and criticisms; to North Park College for giving me the opportunity to prove myself in the academic world; and most importantly, thank you for buying this book.

CONTENTS

INTRODUCTION

Do you remember the reading groups that you had in school when you were a kid—the red birds, the blue birds, and the yellow birds? I was a charter member in the crows!

The crows were composed of kids who weren't going anywhere. There was a girl in my group who ate paste . . . another guy who always had a funny look on his face . . . a big fat girl who didn't say much of anything to anybody . . . and myself. I knew I didn't belong in that group, but there I was. I was there because I was a discipline problem and a poor reader. The school didn't really know how to handle me.

Take a look around you: how many more crows are there in our society, school systems, and homes who have been written off for one reason or another? The school system in which I grew up simply pushed me along year after year. Regardless of my efforts to avoid an education, at the age of seventeen I finally reached my senior year in high school.

In April of my senior year, a geometry teacher pulled me aside and challenged me with the question, "Leman, when are you going to stop playing the game?" I retorted, "What game, teach?" She said, "The game that you are the best at being the worst." It really bothered me that she was able to see through me. She said, "Leman, I've watched you disrupt classrooms and disturb teachers for a number of years. It seems to me that you really are a leader of sorts; the problem is that you have never used your leadership skills in any avenues other than negative ones."

Shortly after our brief confrontation I made the commitment to go on to college. However, in the first semester of my senior year of high school I ranked fourth from the bottom of my class, so when I visited my high school counselor and told him I wanted to go on to college, his words were far from encouraging. I'll never forget his words as long as I live; he looked up at me over the top of his glasses and said, "Leman, with your grades and your disciplinary record in this school, I couldn't get you into reform school." His remark ended our conversation. I remember thinking to myself as I left, "Gee, that guy is a counselor—that wasn't the way the conversation should have gone."

My counselor had good reason to say what he said, since my S.A.T. scores were near the zero percentile, and I ranked very near the bottom of my high school class. On top of that, I was a discipline problem. With the help of a college admissions center I applied to over 140 colleges and universities, none of which wanted me. Finally, after several attempts, I was admitted on probation to our church's school, North Park College in Chicago, Illinois. (I quoted some Scripture that said something about forgiveness 70 times 7!) Although my first year in college was a grueling one, I went on to establish myself academically, winning academic scholarship honors throughout my undergraduate program.

Someone once said, "If you took all the psychologists in the world and laid them end to end around the entire globe, it would be a pretty good idea just to leave them there." Perhaps those are your sentiments regarding psychologists. We as psychologists might very well expect these kinds of feelings in that we have done a beautiful job of confusing parents.

Although I don't claim to have all the answers, I'm sure you will find this book to be practical in every sense of the word. Its aim is not to teach parents how to parent, but to teach parents how to better understand themselves and their children. Its aim is also to create situations in the home and school that are conducive to mature, Christian growth and learning.

At seminars throughout the United States, I find parents hungry for practical means of dealing with the problems that face today's family. *Parenthood Without Hassles** (**well, almost*) provides successful means for families to discover and overcome obstacles to cooperative living. I trust that you'll enjoy the informal style, the humor, and the very practical nature of the book. At times you'll laugh, and at other times you might even cry.

Thank you for buying this book. Without people like you, there would be no successful books and no successful authors!

1

My Life Changed When I Reached For the Ragú

It was 10:30 P.M. when the phone rang. I thought to myself, who could be calling at this time of night? The voice on the other end informed me that one of our students had committed suicide. I received all the necessary information from the police officer, made the calls that needed to be made, and tried to settle myself back into bed for a night's rest.

I tossed and turned. At 1:45 A.M. I was still awake, looking at the clock. I kept asking myself over and over again, why would a 22-year-old young man take his own life just prior to the Christmas season? Apparently it wasn't very important for John to be alive on Christmas morning.

When I received the report from the police department the next day, I had the opportunity to review the suicide note that John had left. The words were very sad: "I just couldn't measure up to the standards of this world, perhaps in the next world I can do better. I'm sorry. John." At that very moment I knew that John was a perfectionist, a defeated one—meaning that no matter how hard he tried, no matter what he did, somehow he fell short of what he thought he was supposed to be.

Curiosity got the best of me, so I went to John's records. I was absolutely astounded to see that John was a graduating senior in a scientific field. He had never received a grade lower than an A in any course that he had ever taken in his four years at the University! John was soon to graduate *summa cum laude*, and yet he took his own life!

Perfectionism may seem desirable in artificial America today. We are reminded by commercials on TV, "We try harder." We are constantly bombarded with advertisements of all kinds which suggest that one brand or another is indeed perfect, implying that perfectionism is a desirable trait.

Perfection per se, isn't bad. My sister's father-in-law is a skilled craftsman, a cabinetmaker. I had the opportunity to see his work in churches and homes, and the woodwork was absolutely beautiful. It was probably as close to perfect as one could find. Many craftsmen with this kind of skill and God-given talent strive to do an excellent job. Most craftsmen can stand back, look at a particular job they have accomplished, and say, "That's been a lot of work, but I've enjoyed it, and it's just the way I wanted it to turn out." I can live with that kind of perfection.

The kind of perfection that destroys people is the kind of defeated perfectionism that I see more and more in my private practice. The person who cannot accept what he does, regardless of how well he does it, has a need to put himself down. "If only I could have worked on the project for two more years, it could have been what I wanted it to be."

Unfortunately, we see perfectionism in very young children. I had occasions to observe as well as to consult in several preschools. It is common to see very young children beginning to show signs of becoming defeated perfectionists.

Little Mary, age 3½, has been asked by her teacher to

cut out three circles for the bulletin board. After two seemingly successful attempts to cut out the circles, Mary rips the circles in shreds, cries, and leaves the room. Mary's teacher, concerned for Mary and her behavior, follows Mary out of the room and pleads with her, "Mary, what's wrong? Your circles were so pretty, why did you tear them up?" "No, they weren't any good; nothing I do is any good; ask Tommy to cut the circles out." Teacher and Mary return to the classroom; teacher turns to Tommy and asks him to cut the circles out and place them on the bulletin board, which he promptly does. Meanwhile Mary chalks up another defeat in her young life.

The reality is the fact that Mary's circles were indeed fine and suitable for posting on the bulletin board. But this fact is irrelevant to Mary. Mary's perception was that her efforts fell short of *her* expectations for *herself*. Her pushing her own standards so high *guaranteed* failure for Mary. Children as well as adults are very skillful at setting standards so unreasonably high that they are really dooming themselves to fall short and fail, which again reinforces the concept that they are no good.

Teacher gathers her 12 preschool students around in a circle ready to play a game of Duck-Duck-Goose. Most of the children clap their hands and jump with glee, knowing that they are about to engage in a fun-filled activity. "Who's going to be the Goose?" one shouts. "Me! Me!" says another; "No, me." says another.

Timmy, age four, takes a step backward, followed by another step. Teacher, observing that Timmy is withdrawing, goes over and speaks to Timmy and encourages him to be a part of the game. "Why don't you want to play?" teacher asks. Timmy just shrugs his shoulders. "Won't you please come and join us?" He shakes his head no.

This may be just one of many instances in which young Timmy, age four begins to develop some means of protecting himself from the fear of making a mistake, of doing the wrong thing, of saying the wrong thing, of being embarrassed.

Young children like Timmy, as well as adults, are extremely capable of creating defensive mechanisms to protect themselves from being wrong, from making a mistake. We see it in homes, we see it in schools, and we see it on the job. We see people like Timmy, who do not become involved and whose rationale might be, "Well, I can't be criticized for failing if I don't try, if I don't engage in the game or complete the activity." We see others who delay starting tasks or who start many different tasks but never finish any of them.

I remember so well working with Raymond, age 36, an electrical engineer. He was a defeated perfectionist, but after several hours of psychotherapy and a life-style interpretation, he came to grips with the fact that one of the ways he had developed of protecting himself from criticism was by starting many tasks and never finishing any of them.

When I raised this possibility, the expression which flashed across Raymond's face said, "Hey, that's me." He went on to tell about the various kinds of projects he had around his home that were unfinished. His wife lamented the fact that she couldn't walk through the garage because there were radios and TV's and different kinds of electronic equipment all throughout the house. There were countless projects that Raymond was going to finish any day now, but just never got finished.

Raymond made some commitments in his life to change, as he began to realize the protective nature of his behavior. We set up a schedule for him to begin to attack these particular tasks one at a time, with the commitment that he would not go to a second project until the first one was finished. A year later I had the pleasure of hearing from Raymond. He told me it had taken him an entire year to wind up all the projects he had started, but now that the projects were done, he felt better about himself. His wife had stopped her constant harassing, reminding, and coaxing, and he felt so much better as a person. Their marriage was also strengthened by his action!

Although Raymond's case turned out to be very successful, people aren't always successful at curbing perfectionism in their lives. Their lack of commitment stifles them. So many times I hear, "well, I'm going to *try*."

Recently I attended a seminar on "The Origin and Treatment of Depression and the Prevention of Suicide" by the eminent psychiatrist Dr. Kurt Adler, son of the father of individual psychology, Dr. Alfred Adler. Dr. Adler mentioned a client that he had been working with who had been talking about trying to change some behaviors in his life. He stated that he paused and asked the young man to *try* to pick up the ashtray which was close to his left hand. The young man turned to the ashtray and lifted it. Dr. Adler shook his head and said, "That's lifting it up; I said *try* to lift it up!" The young man set the ashtray down on the table and grasped the ashtray without lifting it. Dr. Adler shook his head and said, "No, that's not lifting the ashtray. I said *try* to lift it."

A smile came across the client's face with the realization that *trying* was still one of the ways he guaranteed failure for himself. He wasn't making the necessary commitment to say *I'll do it.* I've often used that same experiment with people in my office and had some beautiful results from it, getting people to a position where they make the necessary commitments they need to effect behavioral changes in their lives.

Perfectionism doesn't always encompass all of one's life. Many times I have seen in my private practice men and women who were perfectionistic people in only part of their life. In their work, for example, everything had to be perfect, but their home, their personal hygiene, and their grooming was far from being perfection-oriented. I found that a good question to ask parents about their children is whether or not their bedroom is kept clean. It's a good question to begin to determine whether or not there are patterns in a person's life which suggest a strong need to be perfect.

I believe that many of the children we have in special education in our schools across the country are perfection-istic people who have such a great fear of being criticized for failing that they don't even try at all. The inability of the school system to recognize and deal with this kind of problem has led to the successive labeling and further failure of our young people, which obviously results in a great deal of loss of human potential.

There's no question about it—perfectionists are created; they *learn* to be perfectionistic people. First of all, they learn perfectionism through trial and error as a very young child. If in a given family one child is going to be a perfectionistic person, chances are very good that the perfectionistic child is going to be the *firstborn* child. Why? Although I will discuss the firstborn child in great detail in Chapter 3, it's sufficient to say at this point that the firstborn child bears the brunt of mom and dad's unfulfilled wishes and dreams in their life. It's a fact that most parents "over-parent" with that first child, setting expectations much too high, disciplining much more strict-ly than with later siblings, calling on them more often than other children for assistance within the home, and instilling in the firstborn children prefectionistic ideas regarding early experiences in school.

Little Kristin, age 3½, anxiously asks mommy what she can do to help. Mommy says, "Well, honey, right now mommy's busy, but maybe later you can help." Kristin whines and cries. Mommy relents, "Okay, Kristin, why don't you go and make your bed for mommy?" Kristin, as a pleasing 3½-year-old, goes and makes her bed for mommy. Mind you, the bed is going to look like a 3½-year-old made it. It's not going to be perfect, it's not going to be like a young Marine's bunk at boot camp. Kristin calls mommy into the room; mommy looks at the bed and says, "Oh, Kristin, thank you for helping me." But as she says, "Thank you for helping mommy," mommy without realizing it discourages Kristin beyond belief. While she's thanking her, she's smoothing out the wrinkles, turning over the pillow, and making the bed in near-perfect fashion!

Many times the disapproval, the "I'm sorry, you have fallen short of mommy or daddy's expectations," is communicated very subtly by actions, and not always by the use of words. Mom didn't mean to blow out little Kristin's candle, but the expression on Kristin's face tells us just that! She felt totally defeated by mom's superior ability. It's easy to see where the defeatist rationale can come into Kristin's life: "What's the use of trying? Mommy can do so much better than I can." It's so important for us to be able to accept a child's effort in whatever kind of task the child might be engaged.

I was doing a workshop with a rather large church audience when a young father asked this question: should he allow his daughter to hang ornaments on the family Christmas tree? I asked, "what's the problem?" He answered, "Well, I'm a perfectionistic person, and I wondered if I should let her decorate the tree and then after she goes to sleep change the decorations so they are perfect, or not let her help at all?" I couldn't believe that statement. Everyone in the room howled, except one person . . . dad. He was dead serious! This kind of perfectionism is destructive in children and probably a main contributor to unhappiness in adult life.

Parents can convey to children in so many different ways that somehow their effort does not quite measure up, doesn't quite make it. Many parents are constantly using the terms "you could have" and "you should have." I call these people "you-could-have" and "you-should-have" parents. Most of these parents are motivated out of love, and most of these parents probably think they are really encouraging their children by pointing out to them that they could have done better, but my contention is that this kind of encouragement really leads to discouragement.

In school little Johnnie has completed a 100-word spelling test. At the top of the paper, in red pencil, a big "minus 3" appears with a circle around it. Wouldn't it be just as easy to put "plus 97" on top of the paper? Again, many of us adults are tuned into perfection, are tuned into always being right and really stressing that the important thing in life is to be right, to be correct, to win, etc.

What can a parent do to curb perfection? First of all, a parent must recognize that he or she may be a perfectionistic person, that maybe there have been ways they have influenced their children into perfectionistic thinking. Secondly, it would be helpful to keep out of situations where you are required to be judge and jury, evaluating your children's efforts needlessly. I get asked a lot, "What do you do when a child brings home a report card with a string of A's?" I usually comment with a response like, "It's good to see, Sally, that you enjoy learning." That's appropriate because it puts the effort right on the child's shoulders and recognizes that the child put a lot of work into getting A's in her schoolwork. It gets us out of a situation where we're really saying, "My, you're a good boy because you got A's." A child who brings home straight D's deserves a statement something like, "I'm sorry to see you don't enjoy learning more; perhaps someday you will."

Young parents need to be aware of the fact that firstborn children tend to walk earlier and talk earlier, and to have a good command of the social graces of life very early. Firstborn children tend to be outgoing and on top of things. It's important that parents don't push their children too hard. I see so many parents who just "know" their child is bright and are constantly looking for a program for their exceptional child at ages three, four, and five! We need to be less pushy in our child's education and *our need* to have the child excel.

One of the things that has always bugged me is preschools using names which really convey to us the hurried, pushy approach to preschool education which exists in some parts of the country. "Kiddie College" or "Kiddie Campus" somehow conveys to me that a child needs to be pushed into precollege, preschool, prekindergarten as a way of getting a headstart, of keeping ahead. I think what we really need to do is be more aware of our parental responsibilities in terms of being a mom and a dad, of having the privilege and enjoyment of having the children home with us as much as possible.

Many parents struggle with the fact of a child's birth late in the year. They have to face the difficult decision of whether to send their child off to school young in his grade or to hold him back a year and send him as an older child.

My advice is to always hold the child back a year, sending the child to the school situation as the oldest in the age group rather than the youngest. Many younger children who are fully capable of the academic challenges of primary grades suffer in later years due to social immaturity.

Always assign tasks to children that can be met. It's never good to give a child a situation that he or she obviously can't accomplish. Some parents choose this strategy to "motivate" their children. On the other hand, not giving a child assignments, or not giving him responsibilities in the home on a daily and weekly basis, is just as destructful because it breeds irresponsibility in the child.

Look for the positive. I commented earlier about the spelling paper that it's just as easy to look for the positive things in life as it is the negative things. If things aren't going well in your home with your child, and you are into power struggles (needless hassles), then you need to communicate with one another: "Hey, we can go on like this forever—why don't we bury the hatchet; why don't we stop digging up old bones and try to start anew?"

Criticism is perhaps one of the most destructive means of warring with a child. Parents need to be reminded that constructive criticism can be good, but it's so important that we keep the criticism *directed at the act rather than the child.* I often point out in seminars that there is a great difference between discipline and punishment. Discipline zeros right in on the act; you can be really angry at the act and yet still love the child. Punishment zeros right in at the child. Too many children walk away with the feeling that they are being singled out and punished unnecessarily. I believe that much of children's thinking in our democratic society today goes like this: if you have the right to punish me, then I have the right to punish you. We're seeing too much of that. Children are indeed punishing parents for real and imagined wrongs.

Don't praise your child. We'll talk at length later about how praise can be destructive in a child's life, but *encourage* your children, giving them decision-making opportunities so that they can have a means of making decisions and learning to cope with the realities of life. *When mistakes are made, be practical and develop a sense of humor.* When milk is spilled at the dinner table, a lecture is not needed; a rag is. Perfectionists take such things too seriously. We need to help our children by *allowing them to learn from their mistakes.*

Be aware of comparisons and rivalries in the family. *Let each child know that he or she has an individual, special place in your heart.* Many times when parents are making comparisons about children they say, "Oh, Harry, do you remember when Susie did that?" You just told little Sarah that what she has just done was already done by her bigger sister, who can do things so much better than she can anyway. So you see, the subtle kind of put-downs that we as parents engage in go by us without our realizing it. That's why so much of the behavior we see in children is indeed puzzling to us as parents. Above all, try to curb your own perfectionist tendencies! *Let children behave as children; don't expect them to be little adults!*

When I think of perfection, I frequently think of a couple that I worked with a few years ago—two of the most contrasting personalities that I've had the occasion to work with. Karin, age 36, was very much a perfectionist and a super-mother of six children. She was still able to keep her home in perfect order; everything about her, including her children, was as nearly perfect as could be. Physically, she looked like she could have stepped right off the front cover of *Glamour* magazine; every hair in place, and very nattily dressed, she reeked of perfection.

Jack, on the other hand, looked like he stepped off the cover of *Outdoor Life*. He could have passed as a sheepherder without much difficulty. Their marriage was a very, very competitive one. Karin would push forward and Jack would pull back or retreat. I really had a very difficult time with this young couple, getting them to see that they were in needless competition. The competition had to stop if their marriage was going to make it.

I spent a great deal of individual therapy with Karin; she began to see that her life was a series of roadblocks, hurdles that *she put before herself*, which pretty much ensured failure. She had expectations and goals for her husband that were almost unattainable, but they provided her with the opportunity of saying, "Jack, you've fallen short, you haven't measured up, you're no good and I don't like it." We discussed the possibility that perhaps beautiful cathedrals were built one brick at a time. Karin had to start someplace in turning around a lifestyle that was totally engrossed in perfectionism.

Her spiritual life, for example, needs mentioning. Karin was a very fine Christian woman, but her relationship with God had to be perfect, and because there aren't many things in life that are perfect, she felt very defeated in her spiritual relationship with God. God, in essence, wasn't big enough to love her, or to forgive her for her transgressions.

Finally, Karin made the necessary commitment to begin to change things in her life. She had told me on an earlier occasion that whenever she made a cake for her family, she would always make it from scratch. When she had people over for dinner, everything had to be color-coordinated; everything had to perfect. The kids' clothing had to match the napkins, candlesticks, etc. The davenport had to be "ironed," and the clear vinyl runner which usually greeted people at the door was removed for special occasions only. People were actually allowed to walk on the rug!

Karin told me one evening with a sigh of relief, "Doctor Leman, my life changed when I reached for the Ragú Spaghetti Sauce." You see, previous to this time she had made her spaghetti sauce from scratch, as she did everything else. She had imposed such high standards for herself that the standards not only frustrated her, but led to inevitable failure. To top it off, guess what? The kids and her husband liked the Ragú Spaghetti Sauce better than her own!

2

The Horse Before The Cart

Little Jodie, 18 months old, had never slept an entire night of her young life. As a matter of fact, she rarely slept longer than thirty minutes at one time. If mom was ironing, she might curl up with her blanket on the floor, close to mom, and fall asleep. But before long she would be up and at 'em again, always into everything. Occasionally mom would try to catch a nap herself. Jodie would snuggle up to mom for a few minutes, then awake and again be into all the things that 18-month-old children can find.

Daytimes went by fairly easily: although there was no long prolonged nap, Jodie was very successful in keeping mom busy with her for the entire day. As evening fell, Jodie's fussing usually crescendoed. Mom and dad knew Jodie needed sleep to get the proper rest that 18-month-old children need, so daddy, like most parents, tried his very best to see that this would happen. But when they put Jodie into her room in the evening, she would start to cry and make excuses—just one more story . . . two more glasses of milk . . . one more potty break . . . and on and on.

Mom and dad, in their late thirties, explained to me that they had tried everything to get Jodie, their firstborn child, to stay in bed and sleep through the night. They tried rocking her and tried laying down with her. Mom vividly recounted the times she would lie down on the floor next to Jodie's crib in an attempt to get her to sleep. They tried spanking her, ignoring her, yelling at her, and taking away privileges. The difficulty with the punishment was that the punishment did not work; it didn't attain the goal they had in mind: getting Jodie to sleep through the night. It also left within them the feeling of guilt about spanking an 18-month-old child.

When they tried tactics such as letting her cry and leaving her in her room, strong-willed Jodie would cry for literally hours, and time after time mom would give in when she heard this crying go on and on and on. If Jodie cried long enough she would eventually work herself up into such a state that she would throw up. This meant that mom had to clean up the room, clean up the daughter, etc.

When mom and dad came to me they were as close to physical wrecks as two parents could be. It was at that point that we began an attempt to communicate our respect and love for Jodie by establishing the fact that Jodie had a right to cry, had a right to fuss, and even had a right to throw up. We decided that her parents could not be accountable for *her* nonsleeping, for *her* crying, and for *her* throwing up. By simply holding Jodie accountable for her actions (the crying and the throwing up), mom and dad were able to get Jodie to sleep all night after three successive nights. They allowed her to be accountable for her own behavior, letting her suffer the consequences of her behavior.

We had agreed that Jodie would be given her treat before bedtime, as well as her glass of milk, her opportunity to go potty, and her one story. The parents began to build in a set routine for preparing Jodie for bedtime, and they followed through beautifully. After they put Jodie to bed, they told her that regardless of how much she cried, fussed, or threw up, mom and dad were not going to enter her room. Very predictably Jodie began to fuss, to cry out for mom and dad. At that time mom and dad were getting ready for bed themselves. Dad did a rather ingenious thing. He wired stereo headphones into their radio, and when Jodie began to cry, mom could put the headphones over her ears and drift off to sleep without the interference of Jodie's crying. The real difference was that mom and dad allowed her to cry and allowed her to sit in her vomit all night long—both really courageous things!

Many times the things we must do to bring about corrective action in children take this kind of necessary commitment and action. On the *third night* of employing the principle that, once the door was closed and Jodie was tucked in, mom and dad didn't go in for *any* reason, Jodie began to sleep through the entire night. They began to see that their firstborn child who came to them late in life was certainly a special little jewel. One of the mistakes they had made as parents was to treat her as a special, special child who always needed mommy's and daddy's involvement. In fact, Jodie demanded this attention in a very powerful way. But finally Jodie could get along without them, making them once again parents with freedom in their own home.

Love and mutual respect are the cornerstones of any good relationship between two human beings—between parent and child, husband and wife, brother and sister. From my experience in working with hundreds of families, very few family relationships are based on mutual respect and love.

In the traditional America in which most of us grew up, there was a definite pecking order, a definite hierarchy, in which everyone really knew his or her place. Kings were better than queens, princes were better than princesses, men were better than women, whites were better than blacks or browns, adults were better than children. The way we have dealt with children in traditional society has really been based upon principles of superior-inferior relationships, and not on mutual respect and love.

I'll never forget my experience as a 19-year-old janitor at Tucson Medical Center. Like most 19-year-olds, I was going to find an executive-level position that paid 20 to 30 thousand dollars a year, but eventually (several months later), I settled on a janitor's position at $195 per month.

One of the things I am still reminded of today when I see janitors in public is that their uniform somehow conveys their place in society. My uniform was a steel-gray color with a long-sleeved shirt, which really wasn't well-suited for the high temperature in Arizona. On one sleeve the shoulder patch had "Tucson Medical Center" written on it, complete with a Saguaro cactus, the logo of the Medical Center. Being a 19-year-old, I could handle that fairly well, but the other shoulder was tough to take. It had "Tucson Medical Center" along the top edge and "house-keeping" along the bottom edge. In between these words was a crossed broom and mop! That was very difficult to handle.

One day my shirt wasn't clean and I wasn't about to wear it, so I wore a University of Arizona shirt to the unit I worked on. An old beastly nurse—I can't think of a better name for her—was the head nurse in this particular unit. She never had the time of day for me . . . she never spoke to me . . . I was always in her way. For one particular reason she happened to notice that I didn't have my uniform on. She then inquired, "Oh, do you go to the University, young man?" and I said, "Yes, ma'am, I'm studying to be a medical doctor and I'm thinking of going into O.B./Gyn work." She retorted, "Oh, well, listen, Alice had a birthday today and Gladys brought in a cake. The girls and I are going to get together in the nurses' lounge at 11:30. Would you care to join us?" All of a sudden I was viewed as the All-American boy who was cleaning floors to work his way through school. I was no longer viewed as a second-class citizen!

How unfortunate that we tend to look at people in this light. I'm often reminded of the fact that when we look down on people, we're really conveying disrespect. Many of us have great difficulty in our interpersonal relationships, especially with those whom we claim to love. We have everybody placed on different levels, but the truth of the matter is that we are all of equal social worth.

As a college student I was asked many times where I worked—what I did for a living. People would say, "Kevin, what do you do?" I'd say, "Oh, I'm a janitor." Their response was usually the same: "Oh, it looks like it might cloud up today and rain." All of a sudden the topic was conveniently switched, and the message was, "My condolences; you're a janitor!" I soon learned to tell people who asked such questions that I was a "floor surgeon." Some were duly impressed—after all, business was always "picking up"!

What does this have to do with child-rearing? Again, most of us as parents tend to look down at our children. We don't mean to look down on them, but many times we convey that they are lesser than we are. Yes, we might be taller, wiser, and older, but we are not inherently better than children. This is manifested by our doing things for them that they could very well do for themselves. *Never* do for your children what they can do for themselves. By doing so, we as parents are conveying disrespect to them.

One of the things that I see and am more convinced of

every day is that children in our democratic society view adults as their social equals. This is not to say that we're the same; we're not, but children tend to see us on the same level. And yet when we punish a child we're essentially putting ourselves above him or her. Think of it in these terms: in order to mete out a reward or punishment you have to be better than another person. We must remember as parents that what is really important is the *child's perception* of what has happened, *and not reality per se.* My contention is that children are punishing parents, adults, and teachers for real as well as imagined wrongs.

Those of us who are experts in the field of child-rearing and psychology have done a pretty good job of confusing parents, the consumers. Psychologists who write in parents' magazines are continually confusing us. One week we have a story stating that bottle-fed babies are happy babies, and the very next issue, we hear, "Mothers, don't rob your child of breast-feeding." The following week a psychologist from a psychoanalytical model might report, "If you breast-feed your child, he might develop a perpetual pucker for the rest of his life and his psyche may be forever impaired."

Parenting is very difficult for us in that we sometimes cannot really see the product of our input and work in child-rearing until it's too late. However, it's safe to say that our early input in parenthood pays off handsomely.

Many of the parents whom I see hold the misconception that if we just love a child enough everything will work out all right. *I don't think anything could be further from the truth.* As parents we need to be *action-oriented:* we can love a child without liking everything he does. In fact, we can get plenty angry at certain things children do and still convey respect and love to them. Too many moms and dads suffer from the "good-parent complex": "I've got to be a super-parent; I've got to do everything for my child all the time without fail."

If you think back to your childhood, you'll see that you were probably brought up in a traditional home. On a winter morning mom might very well have fixed oatmeal or Cream-of-Wheat for you, right? The key question is, *Why?* Assorted possible answers might be: "She got oatmeal or Cream-of-Wheat when she was a kid," or, "It's good for you," or, as some parents have told me, "It's a love pat for the tummy." Well, it's that same kind of mother who knows that Cream-of-Wheat or oatmeal is good for you who is going to know what dress is good for you at age 10 or 11, or what boyfriend is best for you at 15 or 16, or what your future vocation should be.

Many parents I deal with are very vociferous in their complaints about giving choices to children. Some feel that we as parents must take the direction and tell our children everything they have to do. Somehow these parents are stopped cold in their tracks when I ask them who is going to make the decision in their child's life as to whether or not to get pregnant at 14, whether or not to engage in premarital sex, whether or not to shoot heroin into their veins, and whether or not to smoke marijuana, snort cocaine, or otherwise abuse their bodies. We need to be providing decision-making opportunities for our children so that they have a broad, rich environment in which to make decisions that affect their lives. Then someday they will be able to make the kind of momentous decisions that adult life requires of them.

Back to the analogy of breakfast on a cold winter morning: three-year-old Phineus comes out of his bedroom groggy-eyed, climbs up into his chair, looks at his oatmeal, and responds with the word, "Yuk!" At this point the traditional mother goes to the *reward* method as a way of getting her child to eat the food that's put before him. "Phineus, eat your oatmeal, honey, it's good for you." "Eat your oatmeal and you'll grow up to be big and strong like your 97-pound father." "Eat your oatmeal, and I'll put some extra sugar on it." "Eat your oatmeal, and I'll give you a quarter." If that doesn't work (and it usually doesn't), mom can jump to *punishment* as a means of attempting to control the child's behavior. Mom can send the child to his room, or spank him, but will probably end up feeling guilty and not like a "good mother." This feeling allows mom to act irresponsibly as she gives in to her three-year-old.

There's another kind of parent that needs mentioning. At breakfast the permissive parent fixes ham and eggs for Harold, buckwheat pancakes for sister Susie, and oatmeal for Phineus. To top it all off, the old man is having a cheeseburger! In this particular family, children are being taught that whatever they want can be theirs in life, especially if they make somebody else responsible. In this instance mom is essentially a short-order cook.

The kind of parent I'd like to see us work toward is the parent who can say to a child in the morning, "Phineus, Krispy Kritters or Cheerios—you decide." Little Phineus says, "Krispy Kritters." Mom turns to the refrigerator, gets the milk out, and pours the milk on the Krispy Kritters. You can predict what Phineus is going to say: "I've changed my mind, I want Cheerios." If you retain only one thing out of this chapter, remember this: as Oscar Christensen says, *"You can't recrisp a soggy Kritter."* Once the choice is made, it is irreversible; we as parents *must hold our children accountable for their decisions!* By doing so we convey respect and love to our children, and are being good models for our children.

Many parents argue that reward and punishment work. This is true. In our society reward and punishment can work. For example, if you pay a dollar a day to your child to keep his room clean, and you have $365 a year to pay him, he might very well keep it clean. But I don't think that's really what we're after as parents. We don't want the child cleaning his room for the dollar; we want him to clean it because he lives there, because his room is part of the house.

In school situations, for example, the teacher has had a bad day because the kids are out of hand, so she says, "Class, if you'll just be quiet for the next ten minutes, I'll let you go five minutes early." Yes, she'll get through the day, and the kids will quiet down, but the following Monday at approximately the same time of day a mysterious hush comes over the classroom as the kids say, "Can we go early today?" The teacher responds, "No, you can't go early; you know we don't leave here until three o'clock." Then it's time for the kids to retort with, "Hey, wait a minute! On Friday you said if we were quiet we could go five minutes early. Today we were quiet, so can we go five minutes early?" This is only one example of the kind of difficulty we get into when we deal with children through reward and punishment.

Haim Ginott said some beautiful things to us as parents about child-rearing in his books *Between Parent and Child* and *Between Parent and Teenager*. He said something one night that really made sense to me: "CHILDREN ARE THE ENEMY; GIRD YOURSELF FOR WAR." He went on to explain that many of us as parents, overwhelmed with our new parental responsibilities, treat children with white kid gloves. Somehow we're afraid we're going to damage their psyches in some way.

I think Dr. Ginott's remarks regarding children as the

enemy are really an interesting concept. I think of the parents who are in the family room watching TV, trying to watch their favorite program, their three children having been put to bed. The youngest child comes downstairs, set up by the older brother and sister to go down and ask mom or dad for a special treat. The youngest is the least likely to be spanked and if he does get pummeled, who cares? Certainly not the two older kids, they don't like him in the first place! In a way, the enemy is trying to get parents away from that favorite TV program so that they'll again become needlessly involved in their affairs.

One of the reasons parents need to have specific bed-times for children is that we really need to convey to children that mommy and daddy love each other and their relationship is number one! It's a very special relationship, and mommy and daddy need time to be alone.

Many times during marital therapy I have been successful in getting a couple to a point where they will be brave enough to leave the children with grandparents or with a neighbor and take off for a weekend! How nice it is to see that two people who love each other will *back up their words through action* and take off for a weekend, enjoy themselves, and nurture their loving relationship.

David, age 16, came to me with his mom for therapy several years ago. She said that on one occasion as she walked into her room David was behind the door with a lamp cord in his hand. He put the cord around his mom's neck and pulled until she had just about lost her breath. Then he let her go. He warned her, "Just a little longer and you wouldn't be here."

On another occasion mom stated that she was sound asleep when she woke up to the terrible feeling of having someone's hands around her neck, squeezing until she had passed out—and then David let go.

I saw David and his mother for a period of about six months. During this time I learned a great deal about David and his family. David's father was killed when David was only 10 years old, and mom felt very guilty about this, although she certainly didn't have any involvement in his death. Mom explained that at times David was like a "playful puppy," that he was a good boy, although he no longer went to school (he quit going just a few weeks before she came to see me). Mom had moved out of the house and in with relatives, and David was essentially living alone in a big house. He was as irresponsible as you could find a 16-year-old today.

I was looking for something that mom could do within the family that would be completely out of character for her. Things obviously had to turn around drastically if this relationship was ever going to become what it should be. It became evident that one of the things mom had never done was to lay a hand on David. We agreed that the next time David acted like a "playful puppy," mom would be in a playful mood herself; she would haul off and smack him across the face with an open hand, telling him that things were going to be different in their house from now on.

Two days later a situation developed where this became a reality. Mom reported that David's eyes became like ping pong balls in his amazement that his mother would take such action. He turned and cried, running to his room. At that point we began to put mom in authority within the framework of their home. David, an only child, was specifically told that he had the choice of either going to school or staying out of school. If he stayed out of school, he would have to work and pay mom a substantial amount of money per month for room and board. If he didn't do this, he was to leave and fend for himself in the world. This was a very tough statement for *any* mother to make.

Mom stopped doing things for David. Previously, for example, when he had come home late for dinner, he could always count on dinner being kept warm for him in the oven. Now, however, when David came home an hour late one night and asked, "Where's my dinner?" mom said, "It's on the stove." It was on the stove, all right—it was on a plate, just as I had instructed her to do. David's dinner was just left on the stove, open and cold. David put his fork into the potatoes, spit them back onto the plate, and shouted, "My dinner is cold!" Mom resisting the temptation to say, "Well, if you would have been home at 5:30 it would have been warm, etc." merely stated, "That's funny, David, mine was warm and tasty."

David began to see that *the old mom was now changing*, as were the rules and guidelines in their family. Through this kind of *action*, of allowing David to experience the consequences of his choice, mom really began to turn things around. She was regaining the position of lost authority in her family. The Cart had gotten before the Horse, but now she was putting the Horse (herself) before the Cart (David).

Most of us as parents will acknowledge that we love our children, but without discipline, love is incomplete. If parents don't discipline a child, they don't love him, for love and discipline go hand-in-hand. Many times in my seminars around the country I'm confronted with parents who are authoritarian, who essentially tell me that giving choices is not possible. They have a very difficult time accepting anything other than being authoritarian. It's better to be authoritarian and be consistent than it is to be all over the place. One of the things we need to do is to *develop consistency* within our lives. *Children appreciate guidelines*; they need to know where they stand and what's expected of them.

The first few months of a child's life are usually easy ones as far as parents go, (although there is the getting up in the middle of the night for feedings, etc.), but as the child begins to develop there are rarely problems that require any outside psychological help within the first 18 months of life. Eighteen to 36 months is that time when a child develops a real sense of power. Children begin to test limits of parents usually around toilet-training time.

My own daughter, while we were in California on vacation, saw her cousin throw what had to be considered a classic temper tantrum. At the beginning of the week I had commented to my wife, "Honey, Holly is going to show us a temper tantrum shortly." However, we got through the week in Sacramento without a tantrum. As we began to drive home, I remarked, "Well, I guess I was wrong—we're not going to see a temper tantrum after all." No sooner had I gotten the words out of my mouth than the family decided to stop at Sambo's restaurant in South Lake Tahoe for breakfast. Holly began to fuss in the restaurant. Like many firstborn children, if things weren't exactly perfect, (pancakes not on the right side of the plate or something major like that), the problem could work its way into something catastrophic.

The temper tantrum developed, reaching its peak just as the manager brought a balloon to Holly. As he arrived, Holly picked up the sugar container and smashed it on the floor just inches from the manager's feet! At that moment I exercised my parental authority, picking up Holly by the left ear and carrying her to the car under my arm. I placed her in the car and locked the door, and then I came back into the restaurant.

The very first thing I saw was my wife with tears streaming down her face. She was looking at our daughter standing in the front seat of the car, facing the restaurant with her arms stretched out toward her mother and yelling, "Mommy, mommy!" My wife turned to me and said, "Honey, don't you think it's time to go get her?" I said, "Gee, honey, it's only been seven seconds—I think we ought to wait a little longer." We did wait for a few minutes; we got through our meal, and then Holly was able to come back in and finish her meal. I've often thought I was really glad that this didn't happen in Tucson, where I would perhaps be noticed by people saying, "There goes that crazy psychologist out the front door with his kid under his arm!"

For parents, it is difficult to take corrective action in public places. There's a lot of pressure on us not to do anything. We tend to remind, coax, threaten, and bribe, and usually we don't get things done very well by doing so. Have you ever noticed how expertly our children use public places (restaurants, malls, supermarkets) to their advantage? How powerful some children can be!

It's important for us as parents to realize that there is a real difference between punishment and discipline. Punishment is directed at the *child*, whereas discipline is focused on the *act*. It is therefore, very possible for us to love a child by disciplining him and have the child know very well that we love him. Parents may still be angry at the particular act the child has done. One of the best sermons I have ever heard was given by our pastor, Rev. John Lovgren, and was entitled "How to Be Good and Angry." The title says a lot to me—we *can* be good parents and still be angry!

Love and discipline are not only compatible, but they are *essential* for a good parent/child relationship. I try to avoid recipe-like methods in dealing with children, but I do offer the following suggestions to parents: (1) Hold children accountable for their actions at any cost; (2) Be consistent in everything you do with your children; (3) Formulate guidelines; (4) Let your children have input into those guidelines so they have greater understanding of what is expected of them; (5) Be firm without dominating; (6) Use action instead of words whenever possible; (7) Don't be afraid to express your love to your child via words and hugging; and (8) If there are difficulties within your family at this time and you sense that things need to be turned around, *start today* by doing some things differently, putting yourself in authority over your child. It's not only the right thing to do, it's what God has told us as parents to do.

3

Oldest, Middle,
And Youngest

―――――――――――○∩―――――――――――

Have you ever considered how very different each of
your children is from the others? Do you realize that if you
have a serious, intellectual, achieving child in your family,
the chances are that he is your firstborn? If in the same
household you have a rough-and-tumble, competitive, yet
social child, the child is probably the middle child. What
about the helpless child in the family—the one who
screams from one end of the house to the other, "Mom,
where's my shoes?" . . . the child most likely to get away
with murder in the family . . . the one least likely to be
pummeled by parents . . . the one whose pet name is
carried on into adult life? . . . Yes, we're talking about the
baby in the family! Most parents with whom I come in
contact have given very little thought to this fascinating
aspect of child behavior.

Do you remember the day that your firstborn came into
this world? Exciting, wasn't it? . . . It was a very special
day. Will you admit to the fact that you had some
expectations and dreams for that firstborn—perhaps
dreams and expectations that you once had in your own
life, but somehow failed to achieve? Firstborns are in a
very difficult position in many ways, for they bear the
brunt of mom and dad's unfulfilled wishes and dreams.
But they are also in a very enviable position in that so

much of the energies of mom and dad are devoted to the firstborn child.

When we take a look at families we see that firstborn children usually walk and talk sooner than later-born children. We tend to push the firstborn child a little harder, expect a little more of him, and later hold the child up as a model for younger siblings. Even with all this seemingly heavy bombardment by mom and dad, the firstborn child generally enjoys his position in the family. Most firstborns enjoy the spotlight of not only mom and dad, but of grandparents as well.

Many firstborns have experienced the shock of having mommy go away to the hospital for a few days and bring home "that special gift from heaven"—a gift that sooner or later the firstborn child figures out he could very well have done without! With the arrival of the second-born child, the firstborn's life begins to change drastically. For the very first time in his life he is sharing with another little person the affection of mommy and daddy, the limelight he had enjoyed too much. One of the things that tends to keep firstborn children going is the child's realization that even though the baby is a threat, the baby cannot really do all the things that the firstborn can do. The firstborn really does end up having a special place in the family.

However, problems tend to crescendo as both children begin to grow. The baby is no longer a baby, but begins to develop a real personality. As a second-born child grows, gains skills, and learns to talk, the competition usually increases.

The competition between the children will lessen if the first two children in the family are of the opposite sex. With every successive birth in the family, children are affected, because the family changes with each individual birth. No birth seems quite as shocking as the second-born's birth seems to the firstborn child. Many psychiatrists and psychologists speak of the effect of dethronement—the firstborn dethroned by the birth of the second child.

I often get asked at seminars, "What can you do to minimize the dethronement effect of the birth of a subsequent child in the family?" It's very difficult to answer this type of question in recipe-like fashion. However, there are some things that probably merit consideration.

First of all, communication (perhaps an overly-used word) is vital to assisting the older child in the acceptance and understanding of the forthcoming birth. Just talking about the fact that mommy is pregnant allows the child to experience the joy of the baby's development throughout the entire pregnancy. This may include taking a three-year-old to the obstetrician's office and having the opportunity to hear the fetal heartbeat.

Secondly, involvement seems to be necessary. Many times I think that parents, without realizing it, really reject the older child with the birth of a newborn. The child is instructed that the baby is too little to touch, too little to cuddle, too little to feed, too little to do anything with. It is very important that the older children in the family see that they are still very much a part of the family, that they can be involved in the feeding and holding of the child.

It's also necessary for the children to realize that the additional time and energy invested in the new baby doesn't mean that they are rejected or loved less. This is where communication is so important. I think we really ward off problems if we talk about this fact before the child is born. Involvement and communication are the two keys to minimizing the effect of the forthcoming birth in the family.

Firstborn children tend to be achievers and perfectionistic people in at least part of their life. They tend to be fearful of new situations, cautious, conscientious, and reliable. We can also predict that they will conform to standards they perceive to be required in a given situation. Firstborn children have high levels of expectations for themselves. They tend to assume roles early within a family, roles that usually remain constant throughout the teenage years.

For example, if there's a "garbageperson" in the family, it's typically the firstborn child. I can't think of anything worse than to have to take out the garbage for the first 17 years of one's life, but this is part of the plight of the firstborn child. Once roles are assumed by a child in the family and later-borns begin to grow and develop, we can usually predict that the later-born is going to develop in areas where he feels he has a reasonable chance for success. This usually develops in a field where the firstborn has not engaged himself. We see so much of this in families: one child excels in football, while the next male child might very well be an athlete, but chooses a different sport instead. Firstborns tend to be "tuned in" to adult values, tend to be very comfortable with adults; they are very much like "little adults." If they tend to be comfortable with adults, they tend to be very uncomfortable with children their own age.

Much of the firstborn's difficulties center around the fact that firstborn children are guinea pigs of sorts. Mom and dad, being new at parenting, experiment with their first-born child. The second-born or middle child, on the other hand, is usually much more relaxed and has a much more comfortable relationship with mom and dad. While first-borns tend to be loners, you could expect the second-born child to be much more sociable and outgoing.

One of the best sources to give us an idea of the plight of

the second-born child is the family photo album. Notice the 3,000 pictures of the firstborn child bound in eight volumes, and then compare this with the 17 pictures of the second-born scattered throughout the home! It's not that we love the firstborn any more than we do the second-born, but it's just that the birth of the oldest was a very special event in our adult lives.

We tend to overparent, and overreact to firstborn children. Can't you remember as a young parent hearing the baby cry on one of the first few nights the child was home from the hospital? Can't you remember thinking, "I wonder if he or she is alright," and running to check and find out? Compare that kind of behavior with the way you react to your third-born child. It's surely a great deal different!

Second-borns have some real advantages. For one thing, they have an older sibling who has served as a buffer for them, paving the way for privileges for themselves. The second-born has the additional advantage of having an older child in the family to model after. If the firstborn child is very disagreeable with mom and dad, very much into hassles with them, chances are that the second child is going to sense this and is going to make a real effort to be agreeable. This is another indication that the first two children in a family are usually opposites.

We often think of middle-born or second-born children as mediators or peacemakers, because so many times they end up doing just that. They tend to be impatient, social, aggressive, and sometimes rebellious. They thrive on competition and tend to be much more independent than the firstborn children.

The youngest child in the family is the person who is most likely to get away with murder. He's the one who is most adept in getting other people to do things for him, and he is an expert at placing people in his service. The youngest child is in a very special place in that his birth marks the end of the trail. He also profits from having older brothers and sisters in the family. He has a unique opportunity to assimilate personality traits and skills from many people in the family and incorporate them into his personality.

Youngest children tend to be experts in "setting up" older children. They create social situations in which they end up being struck by an older sibling, but then use that act as a weapon. They run to mom and dad and tell them of all the bad things older brother or sister has done to them. Then, they typically sit back and enjoy dad scolding older brother for laying a hand on sweet "snookums," the baby of the family. Youngest children in the family tend to be very social, very outgoing, very manipulative, and sometimes very helpless. They tend to marry firstborn children, or those people who are good at taking care of the helpless.

If there's a position in the family that's worse than that of a firstborn, it's that of an only child. Onlies have no sibling to relate to, and they find that their world is really an adult world, one that can impose standards very subtly on the only child. These standards convey the concept that unless they are adultlike, they fall short of expectations, and are therefore inadequate. However, there is also a plus on the side of the only child: they tend to be very reliable and conscientious people. Not suprisingly, then tend to marry mates that are quite a bit older than themselves. If there is a position in the family that falls prey to the "defeated-perfectionist syndrome" which was discussed earlier, it is probably that of the only child.

It all sounds pretty simple up to this point: *firstborn* children, tend to be loners, achievers, and perfectionists;

second-born children tend to be competitive, social, rebellious, and aggressive; *youngest* children tend to be outgoing, social, manipulative, demanding, and sometimes helpless. *Only* children tend to be very adult-oriented, and are conscientious people.

This all sounds rather simple, but it is actually quite complicated. There are many variables that can affect this pattern of behavior in the family.

(1) *Years between birth of children.* Perhaps more than any other variable, the years between the births of the children have a great impact on the family. For example, in a family of three children, with a 13-year-old male, an 11-year-old female, and a 3-year-old female, we really have a "two-family" family. We have a family of two because of the many years between the 11-year-old and 3-year-old. The 3-year-old is really a family unto herself. She is, for the purposes of our discussion, a firstborn child. Her brother and sister are more like second moms and dads or aunts or uncles rather than siblings. I tend to use *five years or six years* as a starting point for a new family: if there is a five-year or six-year gap between births, I draw a line between the two children and begin to look at the succeeding births as a family by itself.

(2) *The sex of a child.* The sex of the child is a very important variable. The first two children in a family, if the same sex, are usually opposites. However, in a family of two, a boy and a girl, we many times see that the firstborn male really fits the personality characteristics of the firstborn child, but that the second-born child (perhaps three years younger) develops the same kind of personality traits that we would usually ascribe to the firstborn position in the family. In a family such as this we have essentially *two* firstborns—a firstborn male and a firstborn female, each with his or her own distinct role.

(3) *Physical handicaps.* Physical handicaps are a real determinant in the constellation of the family. A child who has a physical handicap is usually treated as a *very special child.* He's usually treated this way by others within the family and by others in society, in school, etc. The person usually affected most by the physically handicapped child is the child directly above or below the child in age. For example, a slightly physically handicapped child in the firstborn position can experience a *role reversal:* the second-born child (perhaps just a year younger) may develop physically more quickly and therefore be much more capable at many basic skills. This obviously causes problems for the physically handicapped child, who is older but perceives himself or herself as less capable of performing the various functions and activities required by life. We also see role reversals for one reason or another in physically fit children who are close together in age. The second child overtakes the firstborn child, the third child overtakes the second child, etc.

I have had occasions to work with families who had adopted children who were not natural brothers. Some problems developed from the fact that the firstborn child was physically a much shorter child than the youngest boy, who was two years his junior. These problems can be substantially lessened by giving the older child additional privileges, such as different allowance, and bedtime, and increased responsibility. Unfortunately, many parents make the mistake of treating all children the same.

(4) *Miscarriages.* Miscarriages affect the constellation of the family. The child that follows the miscarriage is usually treated as a very special child. The parents have had a real confrontation with the fact that pregnancies don't always go well; the anguish and hurt that are associated with a miscarriage can sometimes be manifested

in overloving and making that next-born child very spoiled or pampered.

(5) *Deaths*. Obviously deaths have a great impact on the entire family, particularly for the child above or below the child that has passed away.

(6) *Parents' interaction with individual children*. Perhaps this is so obvious that it need not be pointed out, but the parents' interaction with the child and the relationship which each parent develops with each child obviously goes a long way in helping to form the various personality traits that children develop.

Once a pattern of behavior is established for a child, his parents, teachers, and others tend to expect a child to behave in a predictable manner. Once a role is assumed by a child in the family, it is rarely challenged. The child who develops in a scholarly manner is a good example. If the child beneath the scholar in the family is the same sex, chances are that his or her teachers are going to report, "Susie just doesn't seem to care about school; she'd rather run around, have fun, and play games, than do her schoolwork. She rarely completes assignments on time, and although she's a sweet girl and doesn't give us any real difficulty in the classroom, she seems to be very turned off to academic pursuits.

For Susie's older sister, Sally, the teacher's report is quite different: "An absolute dream to have in the classroom. She is number one; she's on top of everything and gets straight A's." The assumption some would make is that Susie just doesn't have what it takes to do A work. However, chances are that both Sally and Susie have the same capability of doing the schoolwork. Susie has seen Sally very well-entrenched in the position of the scholar in the family, and Susie feels that it would be too threatening to compete with Sally.

In other families we see one child who is particularly agreeable and helpful, and who pleases mom and dad very much, while a child four years removed from the "good" child is just the opposite and becomes the "black sheep" of the family. The child essentially rejects the values of the family, whatever they might be.

In school I see the cumulative record as probably the number one perpetrator of passing along expectations for the new year to a teacher about a particular child. Let's face it—once a child gets a reputation for being a trouble-maker and a poor student, teachers will expect him or her to continue behaving in this way, and will therefore invite that child to continue the maladaptive behavior.

There has been research done in schools in which teachers were given false I.Q.'s of children and were asked to grade them at the completion of the marking period. Invariably the children with the highest false I.Q.'s received the highest grades, while those with the lowest false I.Q.'s received the lowest grades. The children who were given the high I.Q.'s were actually the children who tested out the lowest, and those who were given the lowest were actually the highest! There's a great deal to think about in this area of expectations that we have for our children.

In a typical family of four it would be most common to find different family roles assumed by various children. For example, the scholar role could very well be assumed by the firstborn child, as could the role of mom's helper. There are countless numbers of other roles, such as: the comedian in the family, the athlete in the family, the black sheep in the family (the person who rejects the family values), the artist, the musician, etc.

Picture with me, if you will, mom and her two preschool children walking into the local supermarket to shop. As the children are approaching the door, mom turns and says to the children, "Now don't ask for any candy, because you're not going to get any candy, and if you're not good in the store, I'm going to put you in the car." Now what has mom just told her two children? She's told them that she *expects* them to misbehave, and she's told them that she *expects* them to ask for candy.

What can we predict will happen once the children are in the store? You guessed it! After several minutes of mom's shopping the children come running up to her in the aisle with a handful of candy, saying, "Mommy, mommy, can we buy this?" Her response, "I told both of you that you weren't going to get any candy. Now take the candy back right now or you're going to the car." Mind you, the kids aren't blown out of shape by mom getting uptight and yelling, they're just telling mom that the battle is just beginning, that they're around and will be heard from again.

Where do the children stage the battle? Right! At the checkout counter! Notice how children use situations in which they can benefit from the social environment or situation. The children begin to wave the candy they still have in their hands. Mom is busy trying to sort her groceries and is under duress to quiet the children, so to save herself from embarrassment she gives in to her two children and says, "Okay, you can have the candy, but no more. After this there'll be no more candy."

Now you and I and the two children know that this isn't the end of the candy battle. There'll be more candy, there'll be other days, and there'll be other battlegrounds. But mom has just trained the children, "If you bug me enough, cry enough, misbehave enough, I'll give in." Mom doesn't have to give in *every time* in order to convey this message; she just has to give in once in a while in order to reinforce on an intermittent basis the principle that will keep those children misbehaving.

So many times I have young mothers tell me that they have just finished telling their children not to misbehave because they have to make a very important phone call to the pastor's wife, only to have the children pull a "grand mal" type of temper tantrum, or some other embarrassing behavior that drives mom from the phone to take care of her children.

Notice how children zero in on situations where they can create leverage for themselves. When there's an adult on the other end of the phone, that's leverage; they perceive this as leverage, and they use it most effectively. I get so many people—mothers in particular—who tell me that they have been babysitting their friends' children, and that the children were as good as gold until the mother of the children walked in—and then all of a sudden the children began to misbehave. Why? Because mom warned them not to misbehave, and to be good. Essentially, she has told them, "I expect you to misbehave." You see, the kids are simply behaving in a way in which they perceive mom to expect them to behave. *Always treat a child as you expect a child to behave.*

4

Your Child's Personality

⌒

Elaine, age 32, had been married and divorced three times. She was the mother of a seven-year-old son and a four-year-old daughter. Elaine's first husband was a real rat: he was unfaithful to her and he lied to her; he was a problem drinker, he was shiftless, and he was unable to hold a job for any great period of time. Elaine was an elementary schoolteacher. After four years of putting up with his cheating and drinking, she filed for divorce.

After six months of being single, Elaine fell in love with Gus. Gus looked like he was just what she needed—someone who would care for her and be a good provider. As it turned out, Gus was very much like her first husband, Bill, in that he was unfaithful to her and an alcoholic as well. He had a relatively steady job, but there were times when it seemed like he might be in jeopardy of losing it because of his alcoholism. During the second marriage the second child was born. Elaine continued to work during this marriage, and after countless attempts to deal with Gus's excessive drinking and running around, she again filed for divorce, ending their six-year marriage.

After remaining single for almost two years and promising herself and others, "I'll never marry again," Elaine married Dale, who turned out to be a super-rat. Dale not only had all the qualities that Bill and Gus shared, but he was a wife-beater as well, abusing both Elaine and the children. Elaine contacted me after finally deciding that it was time for her to seek some professional help in learning why she always picked a real loser for a marriage mate.

A life-style analysis was necessary if I was going to provide Elaine with some self-understanding of why she picked three such losers in her young married life. (The life-style interpretation involves subjective reporting by the client to a series of questions regarding the person's family—mother, father, siblings, and the interrelationships within the family.) We established the kind of atmosphere present in the home, as well as recollections of early childhood. Finally, we examined all of the male-female relationships which Elaine had experienced.

It was determined that Elaine's mother was very much the dominant figure in her life—the dominant person in the family. She ruled the roost with an iron hand. A teacher by profession, she hadn't taught since the first two years in her marriage. Elaine's father was a successful businessman, and Elaine's mother was always involved in community affairs—Heart Fund drives, PTA activities, and church work. Elaine reported that she knew from a very young age that she was to marry either a doctor, a lawyer, a banker, or someone else who could be looked up to—someone who had status and the capability of making a large amount of money.

Elaine, the youngest of three sisters, was the black sheep of the family. She was the one who rejected the family values and goals. Her older sister, Martha, married just the kind of person whom mom thought her daughters ought to marry, a prominent attorney in the Eastern part of the United States. Her sister, Judy, married a banker who lived in the same town as her mom and dad.

Mom and Elaine always seemed to be diametrically

opposed to each other. Mom had a need to have her three little daughters in dresses, so Martha and Judy, the older two, complied. Elaine, just to show that she was indeed an individual, had a preference for pants. She recited the countless number of hassles that mom and she had over school, dress, boys, dating, lipstick, movies, etc.

It was only through the life-style analysis that Elaine came to grips with some *logical* reasons for her behavior. She realized that her older sister, Martha, was "Little Miss Perfect," who did everything right that pleased others, particularly mom. She was a member of the National Honor Society and captain of the cheerleaders, and she also worked on the yearbook and was very active in the family church.

Her sister, Judy, was very active in athletics and also sang in the church choir. Although she wasn't a straight-A student, like her sister, Martha, she received mostly B's and A's. Elaine finally realized that there weren't really many roles that were left open for her, so she became the black sheep in the family, thus establishing her own individuality. It was an absolute shock to Elaine when I pointed out to her that one of the ways that she got back at mom was to marry people like Bill, Gus, and her third husband, Dale! She was astounded to see that she would go to such length to show mom that she was indeed different from her sisters. She even went to such extremes that she ended up hurting herself and her children.

You see, this reflected her self-image: . . . she was no good . . . she wasn't worth loving. She married, sought out if you will, just the kind of people who wouldn't treat her with love and respect, men who would take advantage of her. Elaine's behavior reinforced her life theme—that she wasn't worth loving. She continually proved this by three lousy marriages.

One afternoon I recall Elaine sobbing, trying to talk through her tears, citing the many times in high school that she had slept with different young men. I asked, "Have you ever really experienced any sexual satisfaction with *any* male in your life?" She shook her head. I pointed out to her that this was further evidence of the fact that she wasn't worthy of having the opportunity to experience sexual satisfaction with a male. She told me she was disgusted with her feelings about herself, and was sick of feeling like a "sexual receptacle."

It was probably at this point that Elaine began to turn around her life. She made some decisions that were difficult to face. With her new determination, I was confident that Elaine could turn things around. One of the first things that really needed to be accomplished was for Elaine to be able to sit down with her mother and share some of her feelings. Elaine really hadn't talked with her mother in the past twelve years. It was very difficult for her, since there was a certain amount of "eating crow" that Elaine felt she had to do if she was going to meet with her mother.

However, she didn't end up doing that, because mom was very happy to know that Elaine was willing to sit down and talk. Elaine told me that they sat for an entire afternoon and evening and on into the wee hours of the morning talking about her life, and especially her childhood. She told her mother that she felt the same way when she was five and six years old as she did now. She felt very inadequate of measuring up to mom's standards and to her older sisters, who had done so many things right in their lives. She explained to her mom that she felt that this was one of the only ways she could make it in the world, to be the black sheep in the family. She always saw herself in competition with her older sisters, and she felt that competition was fruitless because they were so much better than she was.

Elaine recognized that she needed a father who was loving and supportive of her, a father she didn't have. Her father was very much a loner. Although a successful businessman, it would really be stretching the point to call him a family man. He had very little to do with the children, and when he did, it was always at a distance. He wasn't the kind of father who was willing to play with his kids on the floor, to play games with them and share his time with them on an individual or group basis. Elaine shared with her mom that her reaching out for males, even early in her teens, was an attempt for her to gain daddy's love through a series of relationships with males.

Elaine felt very relieved at finding out that there were some logical reasons for these developments in her life. She had previously felt that she was crazy and promiscuous, and was going to eventually lose her mind. Fortunately, Elaine's case has a happy ending. Several years later she remarried for the fourth time to a man who loved and respected himself enough to be able to treat Elaine with the love and respect that she so much deserved and wanted.

Rob was a widower, age 39, and was indeed just the right husband for Elaine. He met her every need. Elaine and I talked together several months after her marriage to Rob, and she was quick to tell me that she never knew that a sexual life could be so fulfilling and rewarding. For the first time in her life she was able to really communicate with a male!

Elaine's early experiences in life, her perceptions of herself, and her family came together to form her life-style, her unique way of viewing herself in relationship to others. One of the themes we discussed was the theme that Elaine only "counted" in life when she was noticed. Like many young children, Elaine couldn't be noticed in a positive way—by getting good grades in school, by being active in church or athletics, etc.—so she got attention in a negative sense—through misbehavior, through doing poorly in school, through having lots of meaningless relationships with males and thus developing a "bad reputation." Even though this was negative attention, and even though this was really sexual abuse, it was still attention! People were still noticing her, and that was the driving force in her life.

We hear so often that a person's personality is really formed in the first few years of life, and that's very true. Early experiences are very, very important. When I go back and get a first memory of life from a client, that very first recollection is usually symbolic of the predominant life-style or life theme which is apparent in that person's life. We tend to remember things that are important to us and consistent with how we looked at life at a particular age. There are literally hundreds of thousands of incidents that we could remember about our early childhood, but we tend to remember only the very few that are consistent with how we see ourselves in relationship to others.

Perception is really the key word in the development of life-style. For instance, given two slightly physically handicapped children from different families, one child may see his handicap as a real roadblock to success in life. This is probably directly related to the fact that the parents might have treated the child as a "helpless little thing." Now contrast this with a second family with a child who has essentially the same physical disability. The child is treated as a normal child, with the full expectation that he can do anything he makes up his mind to do. This child may very well see the physical handicap as a challenge. He might even reach the heights of an Olympic performer despite a physical handicap. So you see, it's imperative that each child really does feel like an individual in a family. Expectancies play a major role in the individual child's perception of their particular plight in life. *Always treat a child in a manner consistent with the way you expect him to behave.*

We pay a lot of lip service about individual differences in colleges in this country, but I find that for the most part we're intolerant of individual differences. We can accept the fact that one 12-year old is 8 inches taller than the other, but if all the children don't learn to read at the same speed, or else walk, talk, or achieve in the same manner, we have a very difficult time in dealing with it. School systems are still generally designed to expect all children to achieve at the same level. Not many people admit this, but as I see it, that's the way it is.

One of the most common behaviors we see in children is attention-getting behavior. Children have the need to belong to the family; if a child fails to find his place within the home, he'll sure try to find it elsewhere. Elsewhere might very well mean drugs, promiscuity, failure in school, etc. A child usually begins to seek out some comfortable roles early in life, roles in which he can succeed.

We tend to think of attention-getting in a negative sense, but attention-getting can also be positive. The child who gets straight A's in school is an attention-getter; he gets attention in a positive way by doing his schoolwork well. There are all kinds of payoffs and reinforcements for these children—everything from stars at the top of a paper to A's on report cards, as well as parental encouragement and praise in the home. "Mother's little helper" at home is a child who is motivated by attention-getting behavior. The child who helps daddy rake leaves in the backyard is also an attention-getting child. A child is saying through this kind of behavior, "I only count in life when I'm noticed, when people pay attention to me."

It's important for a child to find positive roles in which he can get paid off and receive reinforcement early in life, for if children don't get attention in a positive way, they become attention-getters in a negative sense. You don't have to let your mind wander too far to determine how many different ways a child can get attention in a negative sense: through all kinds of misbehavior, bedwetting, whining, crying, lying, stealing, interrupting, and through no or little achievement in school. If a child fails to get attention in a positive sense, he will move most predictably to negative misbehaviors in order to gain attention and notoriety for himself.

Many times children develop a very powerful means of getting attention. In essence, they *demand* attention. They're really saying through their misbehavior, "I'm going to make you pay attention to me . . . I'm going to be so obnoxious that you're not going to be able to ignore me." Most children I see in private practice are attention-getters, and many of them have become more discouraged to the point of developing misbehavior that is really more powerful behavior than attention-getting behavior.

It is interesting that parents can usually determine whether or not their child is an attention-getter or a power-driven youth by their own emotions. When a particular incident occurs, if you as a parent feel annoyed or slightly upset, you're probably dealing with attention-getting. To further verify this, if your admonition to the child makes his behavior temporarily cease, you're probably dealing with an attention-getting child. If your admonition intensifies the misbehavior or action, whatever it is, then you're probably coping with a power-driven child.

Again, *your emotions are the key*. If you feel like

knocking the kid's block off, you're dealing with power. The child is essentially saying, "Hey, I'm the boss; I'm going to dominate you, and you're not going to dominate me." The child's perception is that you are trying to be powerful with him, and if you have the right to be powerful with him, he certainly has the right to be powerful with you. You see, in a democratic society this logic makes perfectly good sense. If you have the right to punish me, don't I (the child) have the right to punish you (the parent)?

The attention-getting and the power-driven children are difficult to deal with, but there is a child who is far more difficult to deal with than either of these. The child who is really into *revengeful behavior* is a particularly difficult kid to deal with. Most juvenile delinquents are into revenge-type behavior. The goal of the behavior isn't just to annoy or irritate; the aim is to hurt. The child's perception is, "I feel hurt by life or by my parents, so I have the right to strike back." If you end up feeling hurt by a misbehaving child, you can assume that the child is into revengeful behavior. If you find yourself asking the question, "How could he do this to me?" you're probably dealing with revenge. Revengeful behavior is very difficult to reverse. It usually takes much more therapeutic time to deal with a revengeful child than it would with either a power-driven or an attention-getting child. It is always best to consult a professional with a child that has progressed to revengeful behavior.

Many times we see, particularly with young adults, the manifestation of revengeful behavior expressed by way of suicide. This is the final blow, the ultimate means a person chooses to "dump on" a parent or marriage partner. The expression "dump on" is so descriptive of the way many people treat each other, isn't it? I envision a dump truck, driven by a kid, backing up with a full load of manure and dumping it on the parent; or one marriage partner dumping on the other. Too many marriages are dumping grounds, with husbands and wives having become experts in the art of dumping: "If you have the right to dump on me, then I have the right to dump on you."

It's important for us as parents to view the misbehaving child (whether he operates through attention-getting or revengeful behavior) as basically trying to find his place within a group. The well-adjusted child who is behaving in an acceptable manner finds his social acceptance by conforming to standards in the home and school. Because of this positive attention, a child doesn't need to engage in negative behavior.

I'm often asked, "Okay, now I realize I'm dealing with an attention-getter, or a power-driven child, or a revengeful child; how do I deal with the behavior?" With the attention-getting, you can do one or a combination of things that will usually stop the attention-getting.

(1) You can tell a child straight out, "It seems like you really need attention. If you need attention, why don't you come over here and let me give you a hug or kiss, rather than having you misbehave." Or how about reassuring the child that mom and dad will always have enough hugs and kisses for all the children in the family, and that there is no need to compete for mom and dad's affection?

(2) Ignoring a particular behavior of an attention-getter will usually get the behavior to stop.

(3) *Avoid reminding and coaxing the attention-getting child.* This is not easy to do. It's much easier to call the attention-getter three times to the dinner table. Call the child once, and if he doesn't come, don't call again; sit down and eat the meal without him. Let the child experi-

ence hunger as the result of his choice not to be on time for dinner.

(4) *Maximize action and minimize words.* When I ask children how many times a parent has to call them for dinner they usually say three times! They then go on to explain that the first time is designed just to get their attention, the second time communicates that you are getting mad, and the third time (always spoken in a sharp, direct manner) means, "Hey, I mean it, you'd better get here." We need to stop playing these kinds of games, because they're senseless and they teach irresponsibility. They teach children that *mom or dad* will be accountable for getting little Phineus to the table.

(5) Look for times in a child's life when you can give attention by way of encouragement—pleasant times, happy times when things are going very well.

With the power-driven child, a parent *must avoid the temptation to challenge the child.* Our first reaction is usually, "I'm going to make that child do it" . . . "He's not going to tell me that" . . . "He isn't going to get away with this." As hard as it may seem, parents must stay out of the power struggle.

With the revengeful child, you are apt to say, "Okay, if you want to war with me, I can war with you" . . . "If you want to play a power game, I can be powerful too." But we really don't need to go through this kind of hassle. You can say, "Let's lay down our arms" . . . "Let's try to establish mutual respect for one another." Kids are very good about telling us what we need to change in our lives. All we have to do is listen!

Many times power-driven kids just have to be given choices for the direction in their own life rather than parents making all the decisions for them. Again, the *use of action instead of words* is the best way of dealing with a powerful child. A child, for example, who chooses to throw a temper tantrum has a right to throw the tantrum, as long as he is throwing it outside the house. It would be most appropriate, *without any words spoken*, to pick up the child and put him outside the door, locking the door behind him if necessary. Just give the simple instruction that when he's through with his temper tantrum, he is to be sure to let you know, so that he can be let back in the house. You can be sure that the tantrum will subside. It's absolutely no fun at all to misbehave outside the home or classroom. Even hermits need society to "hermit" from!

The shy child probably deserves mention at this point. I frequently see children whose parents describe him or her as shy. I have yet to meet a shy child who wasn't a very powerful person. Children use their shyness as a way of *making* people pay attention to them. I remember a little girl I worked with several years ago who spoke in such a soft voice that it was almost impossible to understand what she was saying. It was several minutes before I realized what she was doing. As our conversation continued, I found myself leaning toward her to such an extent that I had almost fallen out of my chair! She was being mighty powerful with me. She was making me tune in to her so much that I really had to strain to hear her. It was interesting that after I pointed this out to her, the volume of her voice increased significantly.

If a child seems to really be into revengeful behavior, it would be best to seek professional help. A revengeful child is usually so discouraged, so much into revenge, that simple means are not going to be productive in turning the child around.

I would suggest that parents avoid retaliation when revengeful behavior occurs. Fight the temptation to say, "I feel hurt by all this," because saying that essentially pays the child off. His purpose is to hurt, and we certainly want to avoid paying off this purpose unconsciously. Communication is the key to turning around revenge. It would be most helpful for parent and child to sit down with a professional person and begin the arduous task of putting things back together.

There are several other common life-styles that we see developing in children. We see the *controller.* He is a child who states through his behavior that he has to be in control of everything, has to be the first at everything, has to win in everything, has to be the boss in everything, etc.

Sometimes, even in young children, we see the *martyr* life-style. They're not good enough, they have to give to everybody, people can't give back to them, and they must do everything for everybody else. They make excellent marriage partners for alcoholics in adult life!

We see *achieving* as a common life theme in young children. Achievers have to get A's, have to be perfect, have to do everything that's expected of them. Again, it's important for us as parents to see that these life themes are *just expressions of the child trying to find his place in the family.*

Mom doesn't have to give in every time to reinforce these concepts; she just has to give in once in a while. Reinforcement on an intermittent scale will keep children misbehaving. The message is clear: misbehave, cry, or fuss, and ol' mom will give in. What a great way to teach *irresponsibility!*

Children are very skillful at using social situations to their advantage. For example: mom has just informed her children that she has to make a very important telephone call to the pastor's wife. She requests that they be quiet for just a few minutes while she talks with Mrs. Anderson. As soon as mom and Mrs. Anderson begin to talk, the children begin to misbehave to such a degree that mom has to excuse herself, put down the phone, and embarrass herself unnecessarily. The children have displayed their power over mom in a social situation.

I usually suggest to parents who are confronted with this kind of problem in the home that they simply pick the child up, place him outside the home, and lock the door behind the child. This gives mom the necessary peace and quiet that she needs in order to continue her conversation without further interruption. In this day of children's rights, it's consoling to think that we parents do have rights also, such as the right to be able to have a telephone conversation without being needlessly interrupted!

The social situation of being in someone else's home is a beautiful opportunity for the child to be powerful with an adult. Churches are also great places for children to exercise power and utilize social situations as leverage. I've had the occasion of watching parents in the choir who were tirelessly trying to get the attention of a misbehaving child in the congregation through a series of expressions, coughs, stares, minimotions, and gestures.

I'll never forget the time I was called into a Sunday school class to consult with a group of sixth-graders who were giving a young male teacher lots of difficulty. We talked about the need for individual responsibilities in a group setting, and we talked about some ways of dealing with misbehavior in the classroom. One of the suggestions I made to the group was that if a sixth-grader was not big enough to remain in the group in a responsible manner, the teacher had the responsibility of taking the child to his parent.

One of the power-driven children in the group spoke up with a smirk on his face and stated very bluntly that this kind of thing could never work with him. I asked him why, and he said, "Well, my mom is the organist." I retorted that I didn't see the problem. He replied, "Well, my mom is in the church service when we're in Sunday school, so I couldn't possibly go where she is, because she's in front of the whole church." I responded once again, "Gary, I still don't see the problem." Gary's expression began to change as he began to realize that I was saying that if he's misbehaving, the teacher should take him to mom right in front of the entire church!

Gary replied that his mom would get really mad. I answered, "Gary, you're probably right. I think she's going to get very mad, but I'm sure you can handle it." That ended our conversation, and I might add that it ended the problems of Gary misbehaving in class!

You see, we simply held Gary accountable for his actions. We said, "Gary, you've got the choice—you can behave in the classroom situation, or we can take you to your mom, who is legally responsible for your behavior." Regardless of the social situation, and regardless of the embarrassment it may cause, this is the kind of discipline that really works and has a lasting effect on children.

During the past several years I have had the occasion to do literally hundreds of life-style interpretations. It's apparent that we as adults behave the same as when we were little boys and girls. The little boy or little girl that was in us at one time is still with us today in our adult life unless some kind of therapeutic intervention has occurred or unless there has been some kind of traumatic experience.

I'm often asked why I use so many examples of married couples when I talk about the formation of life-style in children. It's my belief that this is one of the best ways of informing people about the nature of life-style—that the life-style we develop as a very young child remains constant throughout our entire life. If we are an attention-getter at age 5, chances are that we'll be an attention-getter at 38 or 39. If we're into powerful behavior as a child, chances are that we'll be into powerful behavior as an adult. If we happen to be a perfectionist as a child, chances are that we'll be a perfectionist as an adult.

Our vocation many times reflects to some degree the perfection in our life. Have you ever thought about the fact that architects, accountants, and engineers tend to be perfectionist people and that they tend to be the firstborn or only children in their family?

As we see life themes or life-styles develop in children that appear to be negative, it's important that, early in the child's life we take corrective action to help the child see himself in better and more positive terms.

5

Responsibility Training

Most parents will readily agree with the idea that responsibility training is necessary for the mature development of a young child. However, as we pointed out earlier, parents, schools, and society in general do a beautiful job of teaching *irresponsibility* to children. Most hassles in families can be avoided through action-oriented discipline in the home. Fighting is the one situation that causes parents the greatest distress and concern.

Ronnie, age 10, and Rickie, age 9, were only 11 months apart and were highly competitive. Much of their time was spent verbally pawing at one another, setting up and putting each other down. I told mom and dad that there was no way they could really stop the fighting, since children have a right to fight with one another if they choose to fight, and are really exercising cooperation in doing so. Most parents are surprised to find out that fighting is really an expression of cooperation, since it "takes two to tango."

I convinced mom and dad that it was in the family's best interest to let the children experience the consequences of their fighting behavior. Mom was very concerned because, even though Ronnie was only 11 months older than Rickie, he was physically superior to Rickie. Rickie would usually end up being hurt if mom and dad decided to let them fight. I assured mom that Rickie could handle the situation. Allowing them to fight was an expression of respect to each of the children. We can assume that with experience Rickie would learn that most of the consequences for him involving his fighting are negative ones. If he chose to fight he might end up being hurt.

Mom and dad and I also discussed the necessary guideline: fighting was not permitted *in the home*. Although children have a right to fight, they can only fight *outside* the home, where the peace of mind of mom and dad and others will not be disturbed. Mom and dad were instructed that at any time the children chose to fight, they were to be escorted out of the home, preferably to the backyard, with instructions to continue fighting and be sure to let the parents know when they were ready to come back in.

It was at our fourth counseling session that dad came in with an irrepressible smile on his face. Then he told me that Ronnie and Rickie had had a shaving-cream war in the bathtub. He said, "I remembered your words; you instructed us to use action!" Dad went in and grabbed both of the children by the arm, pulled them out of the bathtub soaking wet, and put them outside with instructions to continue their fighting. Now Ronnie and Rickie no longer fight in the bathtub!

They still fight elsewhere, but not as much, since the pleasure of involving mom and dad in their hassles has been diminished greatly. Now if one of them gets hurt and runs to the parent, the parent simply says, "I'm sure you can handle it!" Before, when that same situation occurred, there had been lecturing about picking on younger brother and coddling of the younger brother—in other words, reinforcement from the parents for this kind of negative fighting behavior to continue.

Children usually choose to fight in front of adults, or

when adults are close at hand. One of the safest places to fight is in the hallway of a school, where it is certain that children are going to gather around and make noise. Chances are that an adult is going to interfere. I've had teachers tell me that when they've given children the opportunity to fight in the gymnasium with gloves on, without an audience, the children usually back down from one another, taunting the other to start the fight, to throw the first punch, but in the great majority of the cases a fight rarely occurs. We must always be reminded that the purpose of fighting is usually for parental or adult involvement.

I believe that the greatest disciplinary measure a parent can develop is the use of isolation—putting the children out of the home for a period of time with instructions to be sure and let the parents know when they are ready to come back in and behave. This is particularly helpful with young children, as young as two or three years of age.

With temper tantrums, for example, when the child decides to throw a temper tantrum during the middle of mom and dad's favorite TV program, it's most reasonable to pick up the three-year-old and put him outside the home. Even a very few minutes outside is sufficient time for a child to settle down and be ready to come back in. What have we told the three-year-old child who throws a temper tantrum in the home? We've said to him, "Hey, you have a right to throw a temper tantrum, but you do *not* have a right to throw it when it interferes with my TV program. You can throw the temper tantrum outside." *The child needs an audience for a temper tantrum to be a successful one.*

Perhaps the most tempting disciplinary measure a parent can yield to is the use of spanking. Spanking should be avoided at any cost. I often tell audiences that the only good that a spanking does is to relieve the parent of the tensions that have built up in him. I believe that spanking only convinces children that power is important. The physical use of power through spanking reinforces that concept in the child's mind. It's important to realize that even if we as parents try to avoid spanking, there are going to be times when our emotions get the best of us and we do yield to the temptation. It's important for us to realize that *we're not perfect and we're going to make mistakes*.

It's also necessary to draw a distinction between spanking and a swat. An occasional swat on a child's "bummy" is a very good disciplinary measure. In situations where a child's safety is in question, a swat is most appropriate. I think of the two-year-old playing in the street; a swat is a very good reminder that his behavior is a definite "no-no." Swats always need to be followed up with honest communication expressing our concern and love for the child in a most intimate way.

The key word in effective discipline is *action*. Billy, age 11, got a new 10-speed bike for his birthday. Along with his new 10-speed bike came some guidelines and some added responsibilities concerning the use and care of his bike. Billy was not to ride on major streets, nor was he to leave his bike out in the yard; it always had to be put away in the garage.

After one warning of a violation of the family guidelines, Billy's dad did a rather courageous thing. He put the 10-speed bike up for sale. He left it on the front lawn with a sign on it, and after only three short days Billy's bike was sold. Yes, Billy was disappointed, Billy cried, and Billy felt terrible, but dad's action in discipline helped Billy in the long run.

Billy was anxious to get his bike back, so he spent the next two months working, cutting lawns, and doing yardwork and chores in the neighborhood in order to earn enough money to *buy his own bike.* Billy now took care of his bike, the bike he bought with *his* money. He locked it up at night, he cared for his bike, and he didn't ride on major thoroughfares. Billy's dad, through action, communicated his love and respect to Billy by holding him accountable for Billy's decision not to follow family guidelines. As tough as it was for both Billy and dad, both the family and Billy profited from dad's responsible parenting.

I was working with a family in a parent-education center several years ago. Johnny was age 10, his sister Tracey was 8, and their mom was very much into entertaining in their lovely home in the foothills. Johnny's one responsibility was to cut the lawn on Thursday evenings. Johnny was a very good kid, but he was very absentminded and always had excuses for why his *one* chore was not completed.

I'll never forget the look in Johnny's eyes when I told him that from now on if he didn't cut the lawn mom and dad would pay someone else to cut the lawn for him. His eyes lit up at my statement—that really sounded like a good deal—until I said, "Guess who's going to pay for it?" Then Johnny's mouth fell open. We set up a very simple plan for Johnny to be held accountable for cutting the lawn or else *paying for the privilege* of having someone else cut it for him. The lawn was to be cut by 5 P.M. on Thursdays.

As fate would have it, when 5 P.M. Thursday rolled around, the lawn was still not cut, because Johnny was not home from the playground. The mother was to go next door and get the 14-year-old boy to cut the lawn for Johnny. The neighbor boy wasn't home, but mom kept her cool and asked Johnny's younger sister, Tracey, to cut the lawn. She jumped at the opportunity of pushing the big lawn mower! She also loved the idea of being paid one dollar of Johnny's allowance. When Johnny returned home from the playground, little Tracey took advantage of the opportunity to tell him that she had cut the lawn for him. The turning point in getting Johnny to assume his own responsibility was finally reached when he found out he had lost a dollar to his sister.

Several weeks after that I had feedback that Johnny had successfully and regularly completed his chore at his home. By holding Johnny accountable for his actions, and giving him the opportunity of doing the work himself or paying for the privilege of having someone else do it for him, we really helped prepare Johnny for life. That's the kind of life that Johnny is going to experience in the real world, isn't it? At the last counseling session Johnny got teary-eyed in front of the group, and I questioned the reason for his tears. He told me, "I don't like you." I said "Why?" He replied, "Because you're giving mommy all those new ideas."

I often caution parents that before things get better, they usually get worse. The reason for this is that we're beginning to crack the mold that the child has dug himself into; children are usually resistant and put up a good fight before changing. Someone was always responsible for Johnny, usually his mother. She always reminded, coaxed, and many times bribed him to do things. As soon as I attempted to change the course of direction of Johnny's behavior, he would of course begin to rebel against it. He had had it made, with everybody doing everything for him. Johnny had been good at putting others in his service, so why should he change?

Billy, age 10, was whimpering on the davenport when his father tried to console him, asking him what the problem was. Billy blurted out that he had lost his wallet and the three dollars his grandmother had given him for his birthday! Billy's dad told me that his first reaction was to replace the three dollars, since his heart really went out to his little guy who had lost the three dollars his grandmother had given him. *But he resisted the temptation.*

I commented that it was great that he could do that, because we were really trying to train Billy to be accountable for 300 dollars someday, and that the loss of three dollars was certainly worth it in terms of holding him accountable for his irresponsible behavior. Like so many situations, Billy didn't actually lose his wallet after all. He had hidden it, as many young children do, in a very special place, one that he soon forgot about. It was good that dad had resisted that temptation!

So many times at seminars I get asked whether children should be paid for doing chores around the house. I realize that there are occasions when a major chore needs to be done or a child needs money for a particular reason for which the parent could very well offer money, but I generally discourage parents from paying children to do chores. As part of any child's responsibility in the home, and because he reaps the benefits of being a family member, each child needs to have responsibilities that really help mom and dad and other family members.

Along with this notion of chores and accountability comes the *privilege* of having an allowance. Each child in the family, perhaps as early as three, ought to have some recreational budget to spend the way he sees fit. Allowances are probably the greatest thing going for parents, and yet I encounter many parents who fight the notion of giving allowances. To those parents opposed, I challenge them to count the dollars they spend on their children every week!

When specific chores are not done by a particular time, mom or dad as money manager in the home may request someone else to do the job. If he does it he ought to get paid for that specific job, and the money ought to come from the child's allowance. The allowance is usually the only revenue a child has available to him, so you can see that holding a child accountable for doing a particular task, or else paying for the privilege of having somebody elso do it for him, is really what life requires of him. This is beautiful training!

Let's face it—the society we live in is dominated by money, and the allowance gets parents off the hook in many situations. When little Tommy asks for a treat at the local store, mom or dad can turn to Tommy and say, "Sure you can have it—use your allowance." If the child has blown his money in an irresponsible way, the answer is, "I'll see you on Saturday" (payday). There might be fussing and crying, and there might be pleading, but in time children will learn that they must be careful as to how they spend their money. If they spend it irresponsibly, they won't have enough money to last them through the week.

On the other hand, if they want to save part of their money for a special gift for someone else or for a treat for themselves, that's obviously permissible. Many parents reinforce the savings by matching or even doubling the amount a child puts into his or her own personal savings account.

I received a phone call from a friend who was a leader in the Christian community in which he lived. He told me his daughter had stolen a pack of cigarettes from a local supermarket and taken them to school. In addition to smoking a few herself, she sold the remainder at her school for 10 cents apiece.

Her dad told me he had talked with Judy and told her that she had broken the state law and also God's moral law. I asked, "Well, what did you do then?" He replied, "It was 10 o'clock at night, and I really didn't know what to do, so that's why I'm calling you." As we talked, I asked him, "Who stole the cigarettes?" He said, "Judy." I continued, "What needs to be done?" He replied, "She should pay for the cigarettes." I said, "Right; what else needs to be done?" He responded, "Well, she should probably take the cigarettes back to the store." I said, "Yes, there's your answer; you solved it yourself. She needs to be held accountable; she needs to go back to the store, give the manager the money for the cigarettes, and return the unused ones."

Judy's dad was supportive in that he drove her to the store. He remained in his car as 12-year-old Judy faced the manager with the truth. I don't know what school of psychology those managers of supermarkets go to, but I'm convinced they're pretty good psychologists. He apparently spent about 10 minutes with Judy explaining shoplifting and its effect upon the store and the individual; it had a great effect on Judy. The nice thing was that there wasn't any lecturing or putting Judy down; dad simply assumed the role of responsible parenting when he assisted Judy in taking the necessary action that she needed to take.

Along with stealing, I find parents equally concerned about their children lying. Children usually lie for one of two reasons: they lie either out of wish fulfillment or out of fear (fear that if they tell the truth something bad will happen to them). Many times an effective deterrent to further lies requires getting behind the child's eyes, so to speak, and communicating to the child that you think you know the reason for his or her untruthfulness. Most parents tell me they will not discipline a child for a lie if the truth comes out without much prodding; it's a good position to assume.

In my own family I found one of my children lying to me about three times in one week, and all of a sudden this became a real concern for me as a parent. I did something I'm not sure was the right thing to do, but it worked, so we'll consider it in this light. After talking with my daughter about lying but continuing to hear lies, I decided to tell her that on Friday we were going to go to Disneyland. Of course she told her sister and her friends that she was going to Disneyland on Friday.

However, when Friday came and she was excited about the prospect of leaving, I told her we weren't really going—that I had lied to her. She cried and she felt very bad, but in retrospect I think I afforded her the opportunity of experiencing what it feels like to be lied to. I believe that our communication was real and honest with each other from that point forward. She had the experience of feeling that disappointment, the same feeling I had encountered a few days earlier when she had lied to me. This isn't a recommendation to lie to your children; I'm just pointing out that sometimes unorthodox methods can bring positive results.

Parents are always getting children off the hook, it seems. I had the parents of little Susie, age eight, tell me that she was just a forgetful kid, always forgetting where something was or that she had to do something. I caution parents of forgetful children to always think about *the purpose of forgetfulness*. What kind of advantage does forgetfulness bring about for a child? It usually brings attention, doesn't it? It's an effective way of keeping mommy and daddy involved with the child, of keeping mommy and daddy busy with him and doing things for him.

Allowing the consequence of the forgetfulness to take its course is the best disciplinary measure a parent can take.

For example, if the child forgets to take the garbage out, someone has to take it out for him, right? Then someone else is paid for taking the garbage out for young Susie. This is fair, and if consistently applied, this principle goes a long way toward teaching a child responsibility.

In most homes the cleaning and picking up of children's bedrooms is a major source of hassles. There are essentially two ways of looking at a child's bedroom. One is that it is the child's room, and that he or she should be responsible for it in its entirety; therefore, the room does not have to be straightened up by the parents. In this view the parent would never enter the room for any reason, including changing the sheets or picking up dirty clothes. The other view is that the bedroom is a room in the house and is to be kept clean and orderly like the rest of the home. The second example is how I usually view the bedroom situation.

A child needs to learn to be accountable for himself; it's important that we don't do things for children that they can do for themselves. If dirty clothes don't get in the hamper, then dirty clothes aren't washed. When Little Leaguer's uniform isn't clean and bright the way he wants it to be, then he has to live with the consequences of not getting his dirty clothes where they belong. If Susie's dress isn't ready for her special party at school, then the consequences of having to wear another dress or otherwise remedy the situation needs to fall on Susie's shoulders, not mom's or dad's.

I've had parents go to the extremes of getting children to pick up after themselves by throwing away things they find just lying around, actually putting them in the garbage can. There has been many a time when young children have gone out to the garbage area to sift through the rubble to find a shoe, or something else they desire.

This kind of action obviously takes real commitment on the part of parents. My contention is that behavior patterns will really turn around when we take this kind of drastic action, when we get children to experience that we will hold them accountable for their behavior.

Research tells us that 9 out of 10 bedwetters will stop bedwetting by the time they marry! Comforting thought, isn't it? Seriously, bedwetting is a problem in too many homes. I've worked with bedwetters as old as 18 years of age. Again, the general philosophy prevails that we hold people accountable for their actions regardless of the consequences.

The first thing that needs to be accomplished is a thorough physical examination to be sure there isn't a physical problem. In the great majority of cases physical ailments can be ruled out. Then we need to think about the purpose of the bedwetting. Could this be a subconscious way of keeping mommy and daddy involved with the child? You can waste your money on buzzers, horns, sirens, and machines that give a mild electrical shock, as well as an assortment of other devices, but the best method of dealing with a bedwetter is to hold the child accountable for his actions by making him responsible for the laundering and changing of the sheets, underwear, pajamas, etc. Other consequences of bedwetting might be the limiting of visits to other people's homes or overnight visits to friends, grandparents, etc.

Parents need to be cautioned to say nothing about the child's bedwetting behavior, except at the onset of the responsibility-training program. They need to outline exactly what their expectancies are for the individual child and then withdraw from the scene. If this simple approach doesn't work within a few days, then parents need to find other reinforcing events in a child's life that are continuing the bedwetting behavior. For example, teasing by brothers and sisters is really a payoff for attention, and may be all the bedwetter needs to continue bedwetting. Siblings need to be reminded not to mention the problem or ask, "Did you wet your bed last night?" When bedwetting no longer pays off, the bedwetting will subside.

Bedtimes tend to be a problem in many homes. The primary reason for bedtimes is that mommy and daddy need to be by themselves, and in doing so convey that their relationship together is number one and their relationship with their children is a definite number two.

It's easy to send the children off to bed at the same time, particularly if they are close in age, but I suggest extreme caution in this area. The birthright effect should be in full force. The older the child, the longer he ought to stay up. *A 15-minute difference can really make a significant change in behavior of children.* There needs to be a set routine involved in bedtime, particularly with young children: one treat, one drink, one story before bedtime. Once tucked in bed and prayers said, if a child gets out of bed for any reason, he foregoes the privilege of having mom or dad tuck him back in.

I've had parents tell me that with great determination they have quite successfully ignored children who got out of bed by not paying any attention to them whatever. Many times a child will choose to throw a temper tantrum in this situation, *demanding* that mom and dad pay attention to him. This necessitates dad picking up the child and carrying him to his room.

The art of giving choices also needs to be discussed. It's important to be able to communicate *direction* to children. For example, a child who balks at going to bed can be asked, "Do you want to be carried to bed or walk to bed under your own power? You decide." Limiting choices is a good skill for parents to learn.

Parents typically find that with deadlines to meet, children get very stubborn. For example, the child who needs to get dressed in order to get to school on time can be given the choice of going out the door with father, fully dressed or half-dressed, with the option to get fully clothed in the family car.

The dinner hour is a needless battleground in too many of our homes. Parents tell kids what to eat and how to eat it, when that really ought to be a decision of the child. Food needs to be put before a child, giving the child the choice of eating the food or not eating it. If the child chooses not to eat, there should be no lecture and no discussion, but certainly no snacks or treats after dinner. The consequence of not eating *should be hunger*; it shouldn't be any of the traditional means that usually fail to get children to eat. So save all the stories about the starving children in other parts of the world!

If a child is late for dinner, the consequence ought to be that he serves his own dinner, or simply goes without it. There should be no special attention or catering by mom or dad for his tardiness.

Family pets tend to create hassles. Many times I discover that the parents bought the pet for the child without the child really expressing a desire for a particular pet. These same parents have experienced difficulty in having the child care for the pet. I sometimes jokingly tell parents, "Hey, you bought the pet—it's yours. You feed it, and you take care of it." There needs to be *accountability* with the acceptance of responsibility of caring for a pet. If a child has really wanted a pet and yet ends up neglecting it, the consequence should be that the pet is sold or given to a family where the pet will receive the proper care. Most parents aren't able to do this for several reasons, so as an alternative they tend to threaten children with the taking away of the pet. These idle threats only teach children that mommy and daddy's words can be ignored because they fail to materialize.

There's a need to expose children to responsibility training early in life, so that when the demands of the teenage and adult years become a reality, children can learn to make wise decisions about themselves. I often think of Laura, age 18 and a freshman at the university. She came to the dean's attention via several local merchants for writing a large number of bad checks.

After the dean made contact with Laura, he found that eleven weeks earlier Laura had left Fort Lauderdale, Florida, with *ten thousand dollars!* She was told by mom and dad that she was now 18 years of age and *therefore responsible*. They told her to take care of the money. I suggest that she did just that! In addition to a new car, Laura bought dresses and outfits for both herself and her girlfriends. In short, she squandered the entire ten thousand dollars in less than 11 weeks! Laura was, needless to say, one of the best-dressed dropouts the university ever had.

To illustrate the point even further, it is interesting to point out dad's response to the dean's call to Laura's home. Dad's first response was to send her *more* money! He stated in typical father fashion that "her mother had brought her up wrong." After some quick talking by the dean, it was decided that father would send Laura just enough money to return to her home by bus.

You see, it's the seemingly minor responsibilities and challenges which we give to children in the early years that pay off handsomely at ages 16, 17, and 18 with responsible thinking and responsible behavior. A home needs to be a laboratory of life, a time for children to learn about themselves and others in the context of a loving home, so they may have the opportunity to make mistakes, learn from them, and continue to mature in a loving environment.

6

Games
Kids and Parents Play

‿‿

There are a countless number of games children play with parents that are specifically designed to entice and entrap parents into their lives needlessly. Only with the parents' successful withdrawal from these situations can a child really learn to stand on his own two feet and behave in a responsible manner. *Any game requires cooperation of the opposition for the encounter to be successful.* Through cooperation, parents ensure the fact that these needless games will persist.

We see it everywhere: *the power-play game*—in homes, schools, amusement parks, shopping malls, and even churches. A child can exercise power not only through temper and temper tantrums, but through more subtle ways as well. The best way of dealing with a temper tantrum is to ignore it if possible and walk away from it. Better yet, isolate the child, giving him the right to have the temper tantrum but not the right to throw it in the presence of other people. Be careful not to lose your own temper; speak calmly but firmly.

Power by way of a temper tantrum is very easy to recognize. There are more subtle means of conveying power that are very difficult for parents to recognize and deal with. Tears and/or shyness can be used as very powerful weapons. Many husbands admit that the most vicious weapon in a wife's arsenal is to cry in the presence of her husband. Speaking in a very soft voice tends to demand that people pay special attention, doesn't it? Shy children tend to be very good at putting other people in their service. What a powerful source of leverage shyness can become early in a child's life!

Another common game is *the courtroom game*. It's played in almost every family in America today. It goes like this: Jimmy and Joey are fighting in their bedroom. Their voices rise to a point where mom and dad come rushing into the room and ask the important lead question: "Okay what's going on here?" As soon as a parent has asked this question, one child points the finger at the other child and says, "He started it!" The other one replies, "No, he hit me first!"

Now mom and/or dad are thrust into the position of being judge and jury in the courtroom. Many times after parents get needlessly frustrated and vent their anger by spanking their children, the children giggle and laugh as the parents leave the room in a huff. Again, *the purpose of fighting in so many cases is to draw parents into the battle* needlessly. Mom or dad could handle this situation by calmly escorting both children out of the house with instructions to be sure to let them know when they're ready to return.

"Mommy, Billy hit me!" cries Susie. This sounds like *the tattle-tale game*, doesn't it? The only way of staying out of this game is to tell Susie that you are sure she can handle the situation. If a parent cooperates with Susie by admonishing Billy, then the tattletale game will escalate to the old judge-and-jury game. Parents would be wise to recognize and hold the phrase "I'm sure you can handle it" close to their heart and mind.

The *fighting-in-the-car game* is an old game, but it still works extremely well for most children. Children find this game most attractive because they have the parents locked into the situation. One way a parent can deal with fighting in the car is to simply pull the car over to the side of the road and stop. If the fighting continues, the parents need to get out of the car calmly, allowing their children to fight, but withdrawing from the scene immediately. If the children are on the way to a Little League game, you can imagine how soon the fighting will subside when dad pulls the car to the side of the road and sits quietly until the fighting stops! Or mom or dad can say *calmly*, "As soon as you are done fighting we'll proceed to the game."

The *beat-the-system game* is an interesting one. When parents dictate the rules of the family without the necessary input and involvement of children, they lay themselves open for children skirting the rules at every turn. I think of Billy, who was told at age 10 that he was to make his bed religiously every morning. If there was one thing that Billy hated in life, it was making his bed. I remember so well his father telling me with a smile on his face, "Boy, that Bill is something." "What did he do?" I asked. "Well, we instructed him that he had to make his bed every morning, so the last few nights he has been sleeping on top of his bedspread, getting up in the morning and merely smoothing out the wrinkles!"

Billy's comments were relevant. The rule was that he had to make his bed every morning, and as Billy saw it, he was doing just that! When dad told him he could no longer do this, the next morning he found Billy curled up in the bathtub in his sleeping bag!

In the *I've-got-a-banana-in-my-ear game*, children needlessly demand being told to do things more than once. They pretend to have a banana in their ear. They won't acknowledge a question or statement without two or three screams from parents that dinner is ready, it's time to go, or it's time to get dressed.

I have the occasion to drive to Phoenix 26 times a year. I'm amazed at the logic of the highway department. The first sign reads, "First Warning—Construction." One hundred yards down the interstate highway, the second sign reads, "Second Warning—Construction." Finally the third sign reads, "Third Warning—Construction"! Where is it written that we must give motorists or children three warnings?

Parents who are successful at beating this game are the ones who learn to tell something to children *only once*. Give them the responsibility of hearing you the very first time, and if they don't respond to the first statement just proceed as if they heard it! The consequence of not coming to the dinner table on time might be that of eating a very cold dinner.

A good friend of mine always had a very difficult time hearing the alarm clock in his own home. In their 25-year marriage, his wife always heard the alarm first, always got up first, and then woke her husband up. When he was on the road traveling, he was awakened by his little portable alarm clock without fail. In fact, he stated that he even heard the click which preceded the ringing of the bell! We train ourselves not to hear because other people hear for us; other people can get us up, other people can be responsible for us.

The *hey-look-me-over game* is a game that children play to make their parents responsible for the way they look and dress. Again, *withdrawal is the key* to keeping out of this kind of hassle. Allowing a child to dress himself the way he sees fit, and experiencing the consequence of dressing inappropriately, is a sure way to end this needless game. I remember a parent of a teenager lamenting the fact that her teenage daughter screamed and yelled at her when she pointed out that her slip was showing as she dropped her off in front of the school. With much practice she was successful in learning to keep her mouth shut, and therefore allowed the consequence to take place. The teenage daughter admitted at a later date that she essentially used her mom for a whipping post in similar situations.

At a seminar in the western part of the United States, I had a retired Marine Corps colonel ask the question, "How can I get my 17-year-old to cut his hair?" He seemed startled when I responded with "Let *your* hair grow long. What purpose does long hair serve with a father whose hair is short?" Isn't the 17-year-old saying that he is very much an individual, different from his father, and uses his hair length to make sure that everyone realizes it?

Jim, age 16, came home from school and announced that he was quitting school. His mom, a single parent and a schoolteacher, resisted the initial temptation to lecture Jim on the merits of an education.

I told Jim's mom that it appeared he was trying to hit her where it hurt. Since Jim's mom was a schoolteacher, his threat to quit school was a great weapon to use against her. As we talked, I told mom that there was no way she could stop Jim from quitting school. In fact, Jim's dropping out of school might really be an *education*; and it was. For a year-and-a-half Jim worked as a carpenter's apprentice in the real world—a great education, right?

Shortly after Jim terminated his employment, he enrolled in a local community college, did better than average academically, and later transferred to a university. Jim learned a valuable lesson in life because his mom had the courage to let him make the decisions that affect his education and life. She had the courage to remain quiet, and it paid off handsomely in the long run!

As Christian parents, don't we sometimes get out of touch with God, row our own canoe for awhile, mess things up in our life, and then ultimately put God back on the throne of our life? God loves us enough to allow us to make our own decisions, so shouldn't we be able to allow our teenagers to make their own decisions too?

The *nobody-likes-me game* is designed to get parents to falsely praise the child. Responding to what the child says is the greatest way of escaping from the jaws of this particular game.

Little Susie comes in and says, "Oh, mom, I'm so ugly." This remark is designed specifically for the parent to say, "Oh, Susie, no you're not, you're a beautiful girl." Why put Susie and mom through this hassle? Maybe a simple statement like, "Gee, I'm sorry that you see yourself that way," might really be helpful without paying off Susie's negative statement about herself. If a child continually feels negative about herself, it may indicate that professional help is needed.

The *never-never game* is designed to produce guilt feelings in the parent. "You never let me do anything or go anywhere," is the lament of many preadolescents and adolescents. The typical response, "What do you mean? We let you go here and there" is a needless waste of time and energy. Not saying anything is the best way of staying out of this kind of game.

Alan, age nine, asks, "What's for dinner?" "Beef stew," says mom. "Beef stew! You know I hate beef stew! When are we going to have fried chicken?" The traditional hassle begins, "Why of course you like beef stew. Why just last week, etc." A simple technique such as writing down "fried chicken special for Alan" on a piece of paper will usually make him *feel* special and at the same time take the wind out of his sails. Chances are he'll even settle down and eat his beef stew. Remember, in case he doesn't eat it, his dinner should be removed after a reasonable time without *any* nagging. At that time Alan is the recipient of hunger, the result of *his* decision not to eat.

The *public-hassle game* is a beautiful game witnessed in supermarkets, amusement parks, and even in churches. The parent rarely wins because there's a good possibility that the child is going to end up embarrassing mom and dad. Be acutely aware of how children use social situations to their advantage! Children are not even consciously aware of the games they play with their parents.

I remember the case of Jimmy, a seven-year-old boy who had the fear of crossing the street. It originated from a real experience of being hit by a bus on a city street. If you want to try something difficult in life, try going through life without crossing a street! This obviously presented a great problem for Jimmy's mom. She drove him every place he had to go, and it was only through action-oriented, therapeutic intervention that she was able to turn Jimmy around. She couldn't go ahead driving Jimmy for the rest of his life; sooner or later the rug had to be pulled. It was suggested that Jimmy be given the choice of: a) going to school by himself, or; b) staying home from school . . . but he had to stay in bed, because children who stay home from school are usually sick and need to be confined to bed without TV, etc.

With only two days of implementing that kind of discipline, Jimmy relearned the process of crossing the street, riding a bus to school, and being the responsible seven-year-old child he could be. He learned that mom was no longer willing to baby him and play his game of keeping her totally involved with him.

The games parents play with children reflect that our training is largely based upon traditional methods of child-rearing. These methods assume that parents are "better" than children in that one has to be superior in order to mete out punishment or pass down rewards. I've never found that to be the case. As a Christian parent I feel that God loves us each the same—children and parents alike. This is a real problem area for many people who fail to see that parents and children are not the same but have different responsibilities. We are uniquely individual and certainly have equal value. *God loves our imperfect selves; none of us is perfect!* We are essentially all of the same value in terms of our individual worth to Him.

One morning I had the pleasure of watching male and female quail and their six "youngsters" run up the arroyo to our feeding area in the backyard. Father quail perched himself on top of the birdbath and at his leisure sipped water from the birdbath while "ma" quail was down on the ground, reminiscent of a sheepdog, keeping her six youngsters in line. As "ma" quail was running around with the children, feeding, searching for food, and scratching in the dirt, the "old man" quail continued to stay on the birdbath, occasionally taking a sip of water.

I commented to my wife, "You know, to the naked eye, old man quail is lazy and poor "ma" quail really has it rough in life. She's down on the ground with her kids working and slaving while the old man is sitting on top of the birdbath taking an occasional sip of water, relaxing." To the untrained eye this might appear to be true, but as I thought about it, the male quail probably got himself in a good vantage point to detect prey in the area—a cat, a coyote, or another predator.

I often use this as an example to magnify the point that men and women are different, that husbands and wives are different; they are not the same. We have different responsibilities and different roles. So many people seem to get hung up on the notion of sameness—that men and women, parents and children have to be the same. I thank the good Lord that my wife and I are not the same! Somehow I envision that if we were, we wouldn't have the relationship that we have!

I also often think about the fact that throughout God's kingdom the male is larger than the female. I wonder what the reason for that is. Is it not that the man is really the protector, that this is part of his responsibility? So many people fear being protected; they don't want to be protected, they want their individual freedom to do their own thing. You see more and more young married women bolting households, leaving behind the husband and three children as the woman searches for her new freedom.

It's important for us as parents to get our game together within our marriage, to give a solid base to the home that our children are going to be reared in. If we don't have it together as a couple, we're really in for a great deal of difficulty in our role as parents. As every year goes by, our parental tools for dealing with the problems that face us in parenthood diminish. It's very important for us to be on top of things in our families, especially during the kids' formative first years of life. Generally speaking, experts agree that it's the first five to seven years that are the most important contributing years to the child's personality development.

Let's take a look at some of the games parents play with children, and see what steps parents can take to avoid playing these senseless games.

First, there's the *rubber-ball game*. What kid hasn't had the experience of playing this game with their mom and dad? "Hey, mom, can I go out to the park and play?" "Ask your father." "Dad, can I go out to the park and play?"

"Ask your mother." Children must feel like rats running in mazes when this kind of a situation occurs in the home! Let's face it—decision-making isn't an easy task, but it is an essential one! It seems like mom and dad ought to have things together well enough to avoid this needless game. We as adults certainly don't like the feeling of being given the runaround, of going from the proverbial pillar to post, so why should we think that our kids enjoy running from one end of the house to the other? They don't need the exercise—parents usually do!

I always remind parents that if in doubt when asked a question by a child, it's always best to say no rather than yes. It's easier to change a no to a yes than a yes to a no. Furthermore, when you give a child a blanket yes to a question such as "Mom, can we go to the ball game on Saturday, and have a picnic in the park afterward?" you're guaranteeing to the child by way of a yes answer that each member of the family will be well enough to attend, that the weather will be satisfactory, and that the car will be in proper working order. In these kinds of situations a response such as, "We'll see what tomorrow brings" is a pretty good answer. It's really not a put-off, and it's good advice for all of us to live one day at a time. *Avoid promising kids anything!*

One of the most humiliating games I had the occasion to watch parents engage in with children is the *manners game*. Picture with me an adult giving a four-year-old a present in the presence of her mom. Like most four-year-olds, she'll begin to rip open the package immediately. Some children, if they're very well-trained, will respond with an automatic "thank you" as they rip the gift wrapping to shreds.

If the thank you does not come forth immediately, what does traditional mother do in this situation? "Krissy, what do you say to Mrs. Anderson? What do we say to people when they give us a present, honey?" Little Krissy shrugs her shoulders and withdraws. "Krissy, now what do we say to Mrs. Anderson, who was nice enough to give you a present?" Now, again, the point is that parents are trying to teach manners in this particular situation. But in their attempt to teach manners, parents find themselves being disrespectful to their own child. True, the parent is embarrassed, but so is the child, and needlessly so.

I maintain that a parent could handle a situation like this in a way that avoids the embarrassment to the child and yet holds the child accountable for saying thank you. One way would be to take possession of the gift and not let the child complete opening it until after she has thanked the giver for it. This could be done by telephone at a later time, or it could be done by letter or note in the mail. Parents need to avoid creating embarrassment for children in social situations in their eagerness to teach manners to children.

I've often thought what would happen if parents ever treated company in their home like they treat their children. Picture, if you will, the family and guests seated around the dinner table. Mom turns to one of the guests and says, "Did you wash your hands before you came to dinner? Let me see them." "Did you comb your hair before you sat down? Your hair is simply a mess." Why do parents feel comfortable about saying those very words to the people they love in their family, but wouldn't do the same thing to their guests? Someone once said that we need to treat family as company and company as family. There's a pretty good case for that in this example.

There is a tendency on the parents' part to be overly responsible for the child's responsibilities. Parents are very good givers, for the most part. They are always giving,

giving, giving! "Hey, dad, can I have two dollars?" "Hey, mom, would you help me with my bicycle?" It's not in *giving* that parents need more training; it's in *taking*, in letting the kids do things for parents and others in the family. We need to be able to teach parents to be able to take from children.

The *threat game* is probably one of the oldest games used by parents. It can by used simultaneously with the old bribe game, equally as old and equally as ineffective. I frequently challenge parents to just sit and listen to the threats they make to their children. There they are, hurriedly packing up, trying to get out the door on their way to California for the family vacation. Dad yells to four-year-old Kristin, "If you don't hurry up and get ready and get in the car, we're going to leave you home." Can't you just see mom and dad and brother and sister leaving their four-year-old home for the three-week family vacation? We don't even make sense with our threats, and there's no way they can be perceived as real by our children.

It doesn't take children very long to learn to ignore our idle threats. They know parents don't follow through. One of my admonitions to parents is to always think before they say things to their children. If they state that something is going to happen, then be sure to follow through. By not following through, we're really teaching a child to be irresponsible. We're also teaching children that they don't have to listen to mom and dad or do what they say. I'm asking a lot out of parents, but no one ever said that parenthood is easy. It's a real job.

This is one of the reasons why we have a need for parent-sharing groups, preferably within the church, which discuss the challenge of parenting in today's society. I'm glad to be a part of a variety of seminars on different aspects of child-rearing, parenthood, and marriage in churches throughout the country. This is the place where we need to reach out effectively to the community and show the community that the church is vitally concerned about the family and about ways of solving problems in the home.

The *treat-all-the-kids-the-same game* is a dangerous one. Most parents assume that they're really being good parents when they treat all the children the same. *Nothing could be further from the truth.* So many times in dealing with families I find that adjusting a bedtime or a privilege ever so slightly can make such a great difference to a child. Children do not like to be treated the same; they prefer to be treated *differently* because they are uniquely different people. They have different ages, different responsibilities, and different constitutions, and many times in our attempt to treat everyone the same we really end up defeating a child unnecessarily. One of the things I'm most thankful for in my own life is that my parents told me what they thought about certain situations and ideas, but always gave me the ultimate opportunity to make my own choice. That is really the pinnacle of respect.

I remember a young couple who came up to me one night after a large seminar I had conducted. This particular young couple shared with me that it was just in the last few months, at ages 36 and 38, that they had really found that God had a purpose and a plan for their lives. Now for the first time they were seeking His will in all parts of their lives. Their question was, "Okay, now that we have experienced the love of Christ through our lives, how do we get our teenage children to experience that same thing?"

I looked them right in the eye and said, "How old are you guys?" "36 and 38," they replied. I said, "Fine, it's taken you 36 and 38 years to get to the place where you've become submissive and turned your life over to God. Why are you demanding that your children turn things around right now? God loves them just as He loves you; He loves them enough to give them the opportunity to fail, to fall flat on their face. He loves them enough to give them the right to reject Him if they choose to. One of the things you can do is to pray for your children and pray for yourselves. You can be models in your home without ever implying, 'Hey, children, be like us.' Each member of God's kingdom is uniquely different, so you really don't want them to be just like you. It might take them a shorter period of time than it took you to come to terms with things in their life, or it might take longer for them to commit themselves to God's love. Go on and live your lives together as you see fit, and then, with your loving relationship and the change that's occurred in your life, there ought to be plenty of evidence that God is real in your home; that ought to provide a challenge for your children."

Dad spoke up and said, "Thanks, I think we needed to hear that." Because of their newness in Christ they were extremely anxious for their children to share the same joy! God works at His own pace, doesn't He?

Remember that all games, whether initiated by parent or child, necessitate cooperation from the opposition for the game to be successful. When a young couple begins to fight in my office, after listening to them for a short time I'll say, "One thing I noticed about you guys is that you really do cooperate." They always seem startled to find out that I would entertain the suggestion that fighting is really a pure expression of cooperation. When you think about it, it really is—it takes two people to fight, two people to play games; it always involves two sides.

As a parent, watch out for these traps that children lay

for us—don't walk into them. Be mindful of some of the games that we tend to play. There are countless numbers of games! I have listed only a smattering of them. Do your best to stay out of them, but when you fail and blow it and realize it, talk to yourself. Tell yourself, "Well, self, I sure blew that one." Give your children the right to fail. God gives us the right to fail; He loves us, and if Almighty God can love us with our flaws and shortcomings, we can certainly turn around and love and accept our own children with their shortcomings and frailties.

7

Rufus Ain't No Rose

⎯⎯⎯⎯⎯⎯⎯⎯⎯⎯ ⌒⌒ ⎯⎯⎯⎯⎯⎯⎯⎯⎯⎯

One of my favorite stories of all time was told to me by Dr. Oscar Christensen, an internationally known psychologist and a colleague and friend of mine. The story concerns Rufus, who came home from school with a note handwritten by his teacher: "Dear Mrs. J.: Rufus doesn't smell good. Please give him a bath. Love, Teacher."

Rufus's mom, an old, poor, uneducated black woman, wrote what I thought was a beautiful note back to the teacher: "Dear Teacher: Rufus ain't no rose; don't smell 'im, learn 'im."

Somehow this story conveys to me where we are today with education. Parents are frequently pointing their fingers at the school, and the school is frequently pointing its fingers at the family. There's very little evidence that there is an effective cooperative effort between the home and the school. This lack of cooperation only compounds the difficulty in dealing with the individual problems of many schoolchildren.

The school system generally teaches our children how to be *irresponsible*. The children are no longer held accountable for their actions, and they encounter very little decision-making within the educational process.

Schools, teachers, and administrators are just beginning to make strides toward democratic teaching methods.

The idea of *social promotion* has been a great contributor to the problem of irresponsibility. To complicate matters, the teachers are instructed very well in the mechanical aspects of teaching (with scores of methodology courses) but are afforded very little education concerning child behavior.

Can you imagine how difficult a position it is for a teacher to be in a classroom all day with 25 to 35 children and not be equipped with appropriate skills to deal with each individual student as a person? We are really asking teachers to function as child psychologists.

In the past seven years I have had the opportunity of teaching elementary and secondary teachers, as well as counselors, concerning the use of problem-solving techniques in the classroom. Teachers are absolutely hungry for effective behavioral techniques. Parents, on the other hand, are just as anxious to learn new ways of establishing mutual respect within their home.

Most parents are equally hungry for a means of creating a healthy relationship between the home and the school. It seems that too many parents are running interference for students by way of their several trips to the school for parent/teacher conferences. The responsibility for school needs to be put squarely on the shoulders of the youngsters. Again, where parents get in trouble is the fact that they assume that stepping in for a child is really helping him.

A friend of mine with a master's degree used to do his fifth-grader's assignments for him. The only thing that upset him was the fact that he got B's and not A's on his assignments! Most of the time we can really help a child by not doing anything that the child could do for himself. Let the child stand on his own two feet and accept the consequences of his behavior.

The first premise a parent must understand and implement is the fact that no one can learn for another person. Many children tell us straight out, "You can't make me learn," and they are right. A parent can't *make* a child do anything, a teacher can't *make* a child do anything, and a husband can't *make* a wife do anything. The only changes we are really able to effect are those that pertain to our own personal life. My contention is that in changing our behavior and our relationship with our child, we can provide a healthy environment for the child so that he can more readily come to grips with life and make productive decisions leading to mature understanding and growth.

Mike, age 10, had a terrible time getting up in the morning for school. As the school year progressed, mom became more and more accountable for Mike's getting up and getting off to school on time. She began with a series of calls to Mike, a series of reminders that if Mike didn't hurry up he'd be late for school. I pointed out to mom that there was no need for Mike to be responsible for himself *since she was doing such a great job of being responsible for him*. At a later session, mom made the necessary commitment to stop playing this unnecessary game. She bought an alarm clock and very matter of factly gave him the instructions that he would have to be accountable for setting the clock and getting himself off to school.

I remember her telling me that she sat in the living room just *knowing* that her son was not going to get up; it wasn't going to work. However, she fought the temptation to go in, doublecheck, and give him one more chance. Finally, at 8:27 A.M., Michael came flying out of his room half-dressed and ran off to catch the 8:30 A.M. school bus. Mom had the previous day contacted Mike's teacher and by prearrangement agreed that if Mike was late to class, he would be given the opportunity to make up the time during recess. This kind of cooperative discipline is the kind of discipline that we need to create within the school system. There needs to be this kind of working together to bring about positive, corrective change within individual students.

If Mike was late for school, the teacher was to say to him, "I'm sorry you're late for school, but how fortunate it is that we have the recess period where you can make up the time you missed this morning." This kind of discipline works. *It keeps the responsibility right where it belongs—on Mike's shoulders, and not on mom's.* Without commitment and action on mom's part, Mike would still be lying in bed every morning, getting his mom to play the unnecessary game that she was accountable for getting him up in the morning to go to school.

Action is always the key to effective discipline. I can't help but think that Jesus Christ Himself was a man of contemplation and action. Do you remember the account of Jesus when He walked into the Temple and saw the moneychangers there on the Sabbath? What did He do? Did He look at the moneychangers and say, "Gee, fellas, I see you're here on the Sabbath, have a nice day!" No! He picked them up and threw them out. He turned over the tables. He used action while minimizing His words. (See Matthew 21:12 and Mark 11:15.) If a rug needs to be pulled from under a child, pull the rug and let him tumble. Doing the unexpected can set the stage for unbelievable behavioral changes in children.

School problems, for various reasons, tend to come to the surface around the fourth grade and again at junior high. Many parents report that the communication they thought they had with their youngster really diminishes at these two mileposts. Have you ever had the experience of asking your child where he's been, only to have him reply, "Out." You retort, "What did you do?" and he says, "Nothing." I'm afraid these kinds of answers are too commonplace. They convey to us as parents and adults that kids are really not interested in talking with us.

Speaking of communication, a pastor paid a visit to a Sunday school class and quizzed one of the kids on the day's lesson. The pastor asked, "Who knocked down the walls of Jericho?" "Not me, Reverend," the boy replied. "I wasn't even there." The pastor then mentioned the incident to the teacher, who defended the boy vehemently. "Jimmy's a good boy, Reverend. If he said he didn't do it, I believe him." Somewhat upset by what was going on in the classroom, the pastor took the matter to the board of deacons. After mulling it over, the board sent this reply: "We feel we should accept Jimmy's word and make no further accusations. The board will pay for the damages to the wall and charge it off to vandalism." If parents really want to communicate with their children they must always be in a position to *listen* to them. What they think is important.

The *achieving* child gets very little attention from writers such as myself, largely due to the fact that most experts assume that the achieving child has no problems. He's doing what parents want him to do. To take exception to this, the achieving child (probably the firstborn child) tends to be an overlearner. Rote memorization is the key to his or her getting good grades. Real academic learning and social learning may not be occurring. A child might be getting the straight A's that somehow we as the adult society convey to the child is so very important. Our competitive society conveys always to be better or best—to be successful. Too many children getting B's and C's are being told by parents that they could do much better. But remember that the child getting B's and C's might be learning a great deal more than the straight-A student!

In most families the first two children in the family are opposites, particularly if they happen to be of the same sex. This usually presents a problem when it comes to matters pertaining to school. One of the most common questions I'm asked at seminars is, "What do you do when your oldest child brings home straight A's and the child directly behind him brings home straight D's?"

It's important for us as parents to place the responsibility squarely on the child's shoulders. I often tell parents that a simple comment such as, "My, it's good to see you enjoy learning!" is a beautiful remark to give a child who has earned straight A's, or else, "Gee, that really must have been a lot of work to get all A's . . . I'll bet you're really proud of yourself." Put the emphasis where it belongs—squarely on the child's shoulders.

On the other hand, the child with straight D's can be told very matter-of-factly that you're sorry to see that *he* doesn't enjoy learning more, but perhaps in the future he will. What's important is that we haven't said to the straight-A student, "My, you're a good boy! Mommy and daddy love you and hold you in high esteem *because* you got good grades." Have you ever thought about how destructive praise can be to a child? It really conveys to a child that he is praised because he did something so well, which in turn conveys to a child that he must always do that well in order to be held in high esteem. *Praise creates a pressure situation for children.*

At seminars I often pick out someone who is very nattily dressed and say, "What would you say if I told you that you looked absolutely beautiful this evening?" If the person I question is extremely well-trained, he or she might respond with a "thank you." On the other hand, most people whom you single out and praise will usually deny that praise. A woman might say, "Oh, this old thing?" Although she had probably bought it just three days prior, she begins to make excuses for the way she looks. Notice what happens next time you praise someone. Step back and see what his or her reaction is.

Many students and children work for praise; they need the carrot before them at every turn. However, I seriously question the merit of such a system. Do we want our children to go from pillar to post always seeking out the next carrot, the next reward, or do we want them to learn so that they can become a better person in this society? Grades per se are really not that important.

One of the reasons children find it very hard to accept praise about themselves is the fact that they hold the level of expectation for themselves so high. It's important for a child to feel that wherever he's at, he's loved by his parents. It's not because he gets straight A's that we love him, is it? Doesn't God love us whether we get straight A's in life or not? We can get caught up in thinking that all a child needs in life is a good education and good grades.

Negative praise really focuses on the child. "My, you're a good boy because of this, that, or the other thing." The use of encouragement, however, focuses on the *actions* of the child. For example, mom walks into the kitchen and unexpectedly sees that the dishes are all cleaned and put away and the kitchen is in tip-top condition. Mother, wanting to praise her child, might call 10-year-old Jack into the room and say, "Jack, what a good boy! Mommy's so proud of you! Thank you! I was so tired. You're such a good boy. Mom is so happy, here's a dollar." Now that's the kind of praise which is destructive.

I'd like to see mom come home, look at the clean dishes and kitchen, and say, "Jack, come here. How beautiful the dishes look! How great the kitchen looks! Not to come home and find dirty dishes is really a special treat. Thank you, I really appreciate your work." This kind of statement recognizes the *action*, and not what a good boy Jack is. It recognizes *the clean kitchen*. It recognizes mom's true feelings about being glad to come home and see the kitchen cleaned up.

It's hard for us as adults to think in encouraging terms as opposed to praising terms. Why? Because we were brought up in a traditional society, for the most part, one that used reward and punishment to control child behavior.

Grant, age 11, crawls into the back of the station wagon, tired after a Little League ball game. Dad turns to Grant and says, "Gee, I'm proud of you, Grant—three for three, what a great night! You really are becoming quite a little ball player." Sounds normal, doesn't it? Too normal, because it's a praising statement. An encouraging statement might seem only slightly different, but would actually be received quite differently by young Grant: "Grant, you sure look like you were enjoying yourself—it was really fun watching you play. Looks like that extra batting practice that you took all week has really begun to pay off."

We don't want the child to dwell on self. We want the child to someday do for others, to make his mark in the world in terms of servicing other people and influencing other person's lives. We don't want children walking around with measuring sticks, feeling like we as parents or adults are measuring them at every turn. Remember, encouragement comes from focusing on *the actions of the child* as opposed to *the child himself.*

The school "cumulative record" has for too long been a mainstay in passing along expected behavior of students. The cumulative record is a place where teachers can record problems and progress concerning an individual student from semester to semester. You can imagine how the deck is stacked when a new teacher goes to the cumulative record and finds that she has a discipline problem in Scott, age 12. She is already *expecting* Scott to behave in an irresponsible manner. If we expect a child to misbehave, chances are that the child will do just that.

Todd, age nine, a fourth-grader, came to me with his family for counseling several years ago. Todd got U's (Unsatisfactory) in all of his subject areas. He was not only in difficulty academically, but he was also a behavior problem. Mom, a career person herself, spent her evenings working with flash cards and other kinds of tutorial projects for Todd. Todd always needed one more explanation: "Just a little bit more help, mom, and I'll get it," he lamented. But he never quite got there.

When mom made the commitment to stop "doing" for Todd, his behavior changed in a most miraculous fashion. Eight weeks after I began therapy with the family, Todd and mom called my office and left the message that Todd had gotten O's (Outstanding) in all of his course work!

Remember this: *a watched late bloomer never blooms!* If you've got a late bloomer in the home and you've been scratching your head nightly, looking at the ceiling and wondering when this kid is going to turn around . . . he'll probably turn around the day his parents make the decision to stop *doing* for him, and instead place the responsibility squarely on the shoulders of the child. Only then can he begin to take charge of his life.

The attention-seeking children in our school systems can achieve their goal (attention) by either *positive* or *negative* means. The attention-getters who choose a positive route in school are the ones who are involved in extracurricular activities and who do well academically in school.

Those who choose the negative route might very well be the disciplinary problems and the nonachievers. So many parents are surprised and yet relieved to see that the nonachiever in the family is a nonachiever because of brothers and sisters in the family who achieve extremely highly. The nonachiever finds his place in life through nonachievement.

Many parents pay off this behavior by running to his school, checking with the counselor, double-checking with the teacher, and then taking the nonachiever to counselors, psychometrists, and psychologists of different varieties for explanations as to why the child is not achieving. At least a nonachiever has mom and dad involved in his life! The only way we can provide motivation for the nonachiever or late bloomer is to step out of his academic life completely and let the child become accountable for his education.

For too long homework has been a problem in homes. Parents somehow have the innate need to remind, coax, and ask questions regarding homework assignments. My position is that parents are not accountable for homework—no flash cards, no tutorial help of any kind. The school can educate our children if our children want to be educated. It is not help, but simply hindrance for a parent to become too involved in a child's education.

If mom or dad feels that their child's behavior in school is a reflection on them and communicates this to their child, they're really asking for trouble. You see, kids can use their nonachievement as a real thorn in their parents' side. This is a beautiful way of keeping mom and dad over the proverbial barrel.

Speaking of barrels, I'll never forget the time I had two young freshmen in my office who had been involved in the theft of a beer keg from a fraternity's porch. The fraternity, being very partial to beer kegs, called the police after apprehending the two gentlemen and pressed criminal charges against them. The two came to me and said, "Dean, would you please talk to the fraternity members and see if you can get them to drop the charges?"

There was a great deal of satisfaction when I looked these two gentlemen in the eye and told them that for years students have been asking us to stay out of their private lives. I further stated that this was a matter between themselves, the county attorney's office, and the fraternity, and that I had no intention of stepping in and trying to solve their problem.

I think I could have knocked both of them over with a feather! They really expected good ol'.dean to step in and bail them out. Why? Because there had been a series of experiences in their lives in which adults had always stepped in and done for them. They fully expected this, and in fact demanded that somehow they had a right to use me to their end. I denied them the use of myself, and out of respect to them I told them that if they were big enough to rip off a keg of beer, they were certainly big enough to go down and defend themselves in the courtroom, just like any other 18-year-old adult.

Some time ago I worked with the parents of Freddie, age 13. Freddie had just been thrown out of school for the fourth time during the seventh-grade school year. School policy stated that in order for Freddie to get back into school, mom and dad would have to come and meet with the principal.

After the five-day suspension, Freddie returned to school and was told that mom and dad would have to come to school and meet with the principal. Freddie went home and discussed this with his parents, but they made absolutely no bones about the fact that they had no intention of going back to the school to admit him—that he had been thrown out of school four times during the year, and that to put him back in school would be ludicrous. Freddie's parents did a very brave thing. They told him that his education was over, and that they had no intention of enrolling him in any school.

After just a few days of staying home, Freddie became terribly bored. He missed his gang, he missed the kids' laughter, he missed being the center of attention in the classroom. At the beginning of the next school year, the parents (with the incessant pleading of Freddie) allowed him to enroll in another school. The results were very, very good. He didn't have to go back and behave as he would have been *expected* to behave in his old school. Freddie had a new lease on life. He benefitted from the loving discipline that his parents had chosen to use with him. He began to see at the age of 13 that school was really not a right, but a privilege, and that he could no longer use his parents in such a high-handed manner.

Prior to Freddie's return to school, his family had sat down and had a meeting regarding the expectations of mom and dad for Freddie's behavior and academic progress in school. The guidelines stated that he had to have C work or better in order to be involved in anything extra-curricular. On school nights he was not to go out other than on a special occasion. If Freddie's grades were not C or better, he could not participate in youth football, which was really hitting him where it hurts.

In addition to this, mom and dad withdrew the

allowance that Freddie had, since he was smoking cigarettes and marijuana, and they felt they could not help sponsor that kind of activity. If Freddie wanted to do yardwork to make some extra money and blow it on cigarettes, there was no way that mom and dad could stop him. On the other hand, after working so hard on lawns, perhaps Freddie might give a bit more consideration to buying cigarettes with his hard-earned money!

As parents we have a tendency to treat kids with white kid gloves. We don't need to do that; we really need to hit the Freddies of the world right where it hurts—in the pocketbook, in the extracurricular activities, etc. The logic of this is that if their responsibilities are met in the home and school, then they can have the privilege of going out and doing other things.

I remember so well talking to a mother of a four-year-old girl. I had just gone through step-by-step procedures which she was to use when little Melissa decided to throw a temper tantrum. I told mom that she was to pick up Melissa and put her outside the home, with instructions to continue her temper tantrum, "But be sure to let us know when you're through and ready to behave, so you can come back in the house."

Mom seemed to have difficulty grasping what I was saying, for she asked, "Well, can I dress her before she's put outside?" (It happened to be a cold time of the year). I retorted, "Oh, sure, and why don't you make some hot chocolate and give her some cookies, too? I'm sure that will go a long way in extinguishing her temper tantrums at home." Then we both laughed. I think she got the message that the action had to be immediate. If Melissa chose to throw a temper tantrum on a very cold evening, that was her problem, and she would have to deal with it.

It's very difficult to convince parents that school is the

child's problem and responsibility. Perhaps this is so for a number of reasons. There's many a teacher who really believes that the child's school problems are the parents' problems, and they do a beautiful job of "dumping" on the parents. Teachers are experts at sending notes home to parents indicating that this, this, and this has to be done with their child.

I recall a mother who, in response to teacher's note regarding her daughter's problems with the multiplication tables, wrote back a very simple note which I thought was most appropriate: "Dear teacher, thank you very much for bringing to my attention the fact that Julie is having trouble with multiplication tables. We really appreciate having this information and want you to know that we have full confidence in you and the rest of the teachers at the school that you will be able to help Julie develop her skills in this most important area. Thank you very much. Mrs. Carlson."

I believe that parents get into difficulty here because we want so much for our kids to have an education because we realize it is important—yet education isn't something we can do for our children. It's an impossibility; you cannot do it for another person.

The only thing we can do as parents is to provide an environment where mature learning can take place, an environment which says to a child, "We love you; this is your home, this is your school, this is your responsibility to do well. We're interested in what you do, and we're supportive of what you do, but we cannot make you do things—you have to decide for yourself." The sooner we can get a family to that stance, the sooner we can expect behavioral changes to occur in children.

There is nothing more encouraging as a therapist than to see someone really turn his or her life around in short order. I often caution parents when we're dealing with a problem child that if we're successful in getting the problem child turned around, chances are that we're going to see some very negative and uncharacteristic behavior in one of the other children in the family, most probably in the child who is closest in age to the problem child and is opposite in personality. The reason for this is that the two children usually form a counterdependent relationship, so that when one moves 45 degrees, the other has to move accordingly.

Recently I worked with the family of Brad, age 16, and Valerie, age 14. Mom and dad came for family therapy. They had heard me at a local seminar and decided that it was worth giving therapy a shot. When they came they told me they were looking for something practical, something they could sink their teeth into, some new ways of dealing with some very old problems in their family.

Mom explained that she had just about given up. That week the kitchen had become so disheveled that she didn't know what to do. She said she felt driven to seek out some professional help. Mom described Brad, her 16-year-old son, as extremely immature for his age. At 16 he stood only 5 feet 3 inches tall and weighed 109 pounds. On the other hand, his younger sister, Valerie, was 14 going on 21. She was very advanced for her age, and for all intents and purposes she had *overtaken* Brad. In my opinion she was a defeating influence on Brad's life.

I began to offer suggestions on how the kitchen situation and the general untidiness of the home could be dealt with. It was decided that when mom and dad came home from work the following evening, they would take one look at the house and announce to the family that there was not going to be any cooking in this kind of home, since it was far too unsanitary to even attempt to do so. At that point mom and dad would turn around, leave the home, and go to a local restaurant for dinner.

Believe it or not, it took four nights of mom and dad coming home, turning around, and going out for dinner before the kids got the message that maybe they ought to be responsive to whatever the parents' needs were, and to clean up the kitchen! The kitchen was the responsibility of both Brad and Valerie. They constantly engaged in battles as to whose night it was to clean this and that. Mom and dad did a very good job in keeping out of that fight, and in essence placed the responsibility squarely on the shoulders of Brad and Valerie.

After the kitchen was cleaned up by the two teenagers, there was a mild family blowup that was followed by a family meeting. This was probably the second step in really putting things together in this family. At the family gathering they sat down and discussed the kind of responsibilities that each member of the family had. The fact that mom and dad worked was obviously a part of this discussion.

An allowance of 8 dollars per week for the 16-year-old and 6 dollars per week for the 14-year-old was instituted. This allowance was met most favorably by Brad but was opposed most vigorously by Miss Valerie. (This was one of the few instances in which Brad exceeded Valerie in anything.) Brad ended up receiving two dollars more per week than she did. The allowance was to be spent on things they needed, everything from busfare to their own personal needs.

The meeting itself was an opportunity for the kids to make commitments about the jobs they felt they wanted to handle as part of their contribution to the family household. An agreement was made that if a person did not do his or her job by the specified time, someone else would do it for him and would receive a portion of the other person's allowance for doing the job for him.

It was interesting to note that during the first week of the allowance, Brad made 4 dollars of Valerie's 6-dollar allowance for doing things that Valerie refused to do, even though Brad had always been the one who never wanted to do anything. In fact, mom said he was the kind of kid who would just sit in his room and let life go by. He really didn't want to be bothered by anything. On the other hand, within the family he was very argumentative, and the only kids he played with were ones eight years his junior.

The allowance, combined with a job that Brad secured a few weeks later, really began to turn his life around. He began to see himself as a 16-year-old and not as a 12-year-old. Mom and dad were willing to give him new freedoms and new responsibilities, and he met the challenge beautifully. On the other hand, Miss Valerie, after initially getting her nose bent out of shape, returned to her semicooperative state and seemed to make a pretty good adjustment.

During therapy with Brad, he pointed out that he felt like he was really treated like a little kid by his parents, which only reinforced his self-concept that he was small and very immature. It was really fun to watch Brad's personality take a dramatic change for the better.

This change could only have occurred because mom and dad were: a) courageous enough to go and seek professional help; b) strong enough to be able to exhibit some uncharacteristic behavior within themselves (such as leaving the house and going out for dinner); and c) courageous enough to hold regular meetings in their family in which everyone would have an opportunity to share in the decision-making within the family. Mom and dad had been holding down young Brad without knowing it, thereby reinforcing the poor self-concept that he had already developed.

A little over a year ago I worked with a family of five adolescent kids—three teenage girls and two boys, ages 12 and 10. We were working on some of the same concepts that were discussed in Brad's and Valerie's situation when I mentioned the possibility that perhaps the family could meet on a regular basis and the kids could have some input as to the rules and regulations and other things that affect the family. The kids jumped at the opportunity. I cite this particular example because sometimes children with a new freedom misuse it greatly.

I'll never forget dad's question. He said, "Do you mean that each of the kids gets one vote—an equal vote to what my wife and I would vote?" I replied, "Yes." He said, "That's five votes for them and two for us." I said, "That's true, but trust me—the kids will become responsible as you delegate this responsibility to them." Well, the following week dad came in with a smirk on his face, so I asked him how things had gone. He replied, "Well, I'll tell you how things have gone. We used to have rules and regulations at our house regarding what time people had to be home at night. If they were going some place unexpectedly, the children were required to always call us and let us know exactly where they were and what time they would be home. During that first meeting that *you suggested*, the children wiped out all the rules."

Struggling for an answer, I pleaded with dad to please stay with the agreement for just one more session, and perhaps we could make this poor decision on the children's part a learning situation. At my suggestion, the following evening mom failed to come home from work at her usual 5:30 P.M. At around 7 P.M. that evening, dad and the children began to make calls to her place of employment, friends, and relatives, but no one had seen mom. As the hours passed, the kids panicked. They were very upset about what could have happened to mom, and about where she was. Dad played along with the game most beautifully. Even the fake call to the police went ever so smoothly. No one slept the entire evening except mom, who was tucked in a Simmons hide-a-bed at her father-in-law's home.

At 7:30 the next morning mom walked into the house! The kids flew out of their seats and ran to her, hugging and kissing her. Mixed with tears, they asked, "Where were you? We were so worried! We called the police, we called the hospitals." Mom replied, "I thought at our meeting last night we wiped out all the rules and regulations about what time we had to be home at night, and also that we had to call people and let them know where we were."

At that point, Jamie, the oldest daughter, called for an immediate family meeting. Right then the three teenage girls, along with 12-year-old Jimmy and 10-year-old Jackie, reinstated the same rule they had wiped out two nights previously. Why? Because they had the opportunity to see that the rules were really in the family's best interests. Sure, we parents are wiser, and we probably know exactly what the rules ought to be, but if we'll only take the time to let the kids themselves have the necessary input into the rules, they'll probably adhere to them a lot better than if they're autocratically picked out of thin air and put before children as the law.

Whether at home or in the school, when we see misbehavior of a particular child, we must always ask ourselves, what's the social purpose of that behavior? Too many times at parent-teacher conferences, teachers tell parents that little Johnnie is careless, that he doesn't prepare his work carefully. Many parents seem startled when I point out that carelessness can be a child's way of protecting himself from getting A's.

Parents ask, "Protecting themselves from what?" I reply, "From getting A's, because if they do exceptionally well in school, somehow that conveys the idea that they are capable of getting A's, and then they feel under pressure to do so all the time." This gets us back to the fact that we as parents need to be thinking about ways of *encouraging* children as opposed to *praising* them. It's only the most expert and trained teacher who can look at the misbehavior of children and ask the question, "What is the purpose of this behavior?" Only with this knowledge can the teacher bring about corrective discipline that is conducive to the mature growth and learning of the child.

One of the most beautiful examples of discipline I can think of is from my experiences with teachers from a parochial school in Phoenix, Arizona. The Sister who taught this particular fifth-grade religion class one day noticed that two of the children who were present at the beginning of the class had mysteriously disappeared. It wasn't long before the looks of the other students and a few giggles and smiles conveyed that the two children had sought refuge in a refrigerator box in the back of the room.

Granted, the class was a religion class and might not have been the most interesting order of the day, but the Sister did a brave thing. She continued the class without interruption, and then several minutes later dismissed them. She knew what the purpose of the two children was—to get attention from both her and the group. In order for the attention to be really received, the Sister would have had to stop the class, acknowledge their foolishness, and administer discipline. She chose not to do so.

After all the children had left the room, the Sister remained in the room, as did the two children who were still in the box. She said, "Boys, you can come out now." Then she added, "We're going to the principal's office." At this point Sister sounds like any other teacher who doesn't know how to deal with discipline. It appeared that she was going to dump the students on the principal's lap, but Sister didn't do that either. She merely walked them to the office and gave both of them instructions to *call their homes*. That's all she did.

The first young boy got on the phone and said, "Hello, mom, this is Richard. Guess where I spent Religion class . . . in the box," he sobbed. Mom tried very hard to get Sister on the phone. Richard turned and extended the phone to Sister, but she just shook her head no. He said, "I'll tell you later, mom, when I get home" and hung up the phone. The other little boy did the same thing. He called his family, and essentially the same thing transpired. Both parents were anxious to get Sister on the phone, but she kept the responsibility right on the kids' shoulders. She never told the children what to say; she just ordered them to call their homes.

Richard told his mother that he had spent Religion class in the box instead of the classroom seat, which was his choice. He commented later to Sister that his mom sounded really mad; Sister simply said, "Yeah, I bet she was." This kind of discipline is the kind of discipline that we need to have in our schools. It's too easy to run interference for the children and to carry on the conversation only between the adults.

I can think of a couple of parents who did a very courageous thing when their 14-year-old son was ordered to juvenile detention for a hearing about operating a vehicle on the street without a license. They went with

Mickey to the juvenile court center, but when it came time for him to go in and talk with the juvenile judge, they did the unexpected. They sat down in the waiting room and told Mickey they would remain right there, and that when he was through he was to come out, and they would go home. Since Mickey chose to drive his motor scooter in the street without a license, mom and dad felt he was big enough to stand on his own two feet before the judge. In doing so, they prohibited Mickey from using them in any sense of the word. They were just there as parents because they had a legal obligation to be there, but they felt it was best to just sit back and let Mickey stand on his own two feet.

Sometimes within our schools we see kids who are so totally discouraged that they virtually give up. They're like turtles who pull their heads in and tuck themselves neatly under their shell and wish the world would go away. Essentially, they refuse to learn.

One of the most classic cases of this type that I have ever dealt with was the case of Bobby, whom I saw over a fairly long period of time. When Bobby came to me at age 11, the only thing I knew about him was the fact that he was supposed to be mentally retarded. Bobby's mother, a registered nurse, was very much a martyr. She was very good at giving the shirt off her back, but if someone else offered a shirt to her, she would never accept it. Bobby was called "retard" to his face by neighborhood children, and even his younger brother occasionally referred to him with the same term.

I saw Bobby at a parent-education center at which I was teaching teachers and counselors behavioral techniques in the classroom. Although it may sound strange, we worked with Bobby's family in a group situation there. Through past experiences, we have found that the audience, by way of their participation and encouragement, goes a long way in bringing about the kind of behavior changes needed.

When Bobby first came in to the education center and saw me at the front, he walked around and made a series of gestures and unintelligible remarks to the audience. I wasn't sure where to begin, but I knew that what I was seeing was somehow a demonstration of the power that Bobby possessed.

I turned to him and said, "Bobby, is the game over? Please sit down." With that he flashed a dirty look my way, sat down on the end of the bench, and turned his back to me. At that point I commented that I was encouraged because I at least knew that Bobby thought I was the enemy and that I deserved getting his back shown to me. I felt that we had to find something that we could work on—something that would convince mom that behavioral change with Bobby was indeed possible.

We focused on the fact that Bobby soiled his pants regularly. Bobby was in a special school for retarded children, and his mother would bring to the school *each day* a fresh change of underwear and pants. Bobby would be sent to the nurse when he soiled his pants, and he would then be changed, cleaned up, and returned to the classroom.

I turned to Bobby during the session and asked him if something had found its way into his pants which did not belong there on a daily basis. He looked at me sort of strangely, so I continued, "You know what I mean. You soil your pants, don't you?" He refused to answer, so I said, "Bobby, since you are now 11 years old, we think you ought to be responsible enough to make sure this doesn't happen; from now on, if you choose to soil your pant, you're going to sit in them. Mom is not going to be in school with a clean change of clothes, and we're not going to continue this kind of nonsense any further."

What have I just said to Bobby? I've said that I respect him because we're giving him the choice to either soil his pants or not. We've also stopped reinforcing his negative behavior (soiling his pants). Mom's trips to school and her special attention were just another way that Bobby was able to keep his mother unnecessarily involved in his life.

I don't know what you think of peer pressure, but peer pressure in school, even a school for retarded children, is very strong. The other children did not like the aroma that emerged from Bobby's seat, and in just two days the soiling behavior stopped. It was at this point that mom saw that for 11 years she had been paying off this irresponsible behavior.

Bobby's case is really a classic one, because when he had been about 18 months old he had suffered a fall, and a medical doctor had happened to use the term "mental retardation" in a description of Bobby's injuries. As best as I can determine, he only used that term in passing, but the interesting thing is that mom and dad at that point began to treat Bobby as a mentally retarded child, doing almost everything for him. He was robbed of the responsibility of doing anything, including the responsibility of controlling his own bowels. They literally raised Bobby to be a mentally retarded child!

At the end of the therapy, Bobby came into the parent-education center and went through one of his sports scrapbooks, describing all the players on the team and what they had done over the past year. His speech was a thousand percent better, and we were all able to understand him. The good news is that today Bobby lives a normal life. He graduated from public high school, and the last information I had was that he was enrolled in a community college and was doing quite well.

Occasionally we run into a classic situation like Bobby's, in which the kinds of behavioral changes that are made are absolutely unbelievable. The point is that until commitment comes from parents to effect behavioral change, behavioral change will not occur. We have to give children the right to make decisions for themselves that affect their own lives.

School is the child's problem. I know that PTA's encourage a wonderful working relationship between the home and the school, but I have not yet found a PTA that has a wonderful working relationship with parents! Nor do I find teachers who have wonderful working relationships with parents. Instead, I find teachers who are frustrated because they don't know how to deal with children behaviorally in the classroom, so they point the finger to the home and say, "It's the home's problem, you take care of it." On the other hand, I find lots of parents who do the same kind of buck-passing. When they have problems with their children they say, "It's the school's fault—they're not teaching my kid to be responsible."

There are times when home and school can work together in a most responsible way that will lead to a child's mature growth and learning. In order for a child to get anything out of his education, the basic posture for a parent is a position that says, "We're here, we love you, we support you; school is your thing, your grades reflect what you have learned, your behavior reflects the kind of person you are, etc."

We can't make a child learn, and we can't make a child behave in his school situation. The only thing we can do is to hold him accountable for his decision to not do well in school, or to behave in an unruly manner in school. One of the most difficult things for parents to learn seems to be the ability to keep their mouth shut and not say anything. This is difficult because we're wiser, we have more knowledge, and we have more experience. But children *need the right to fail*. They need the right to fall flat on their face, to pick themselves up and go on.

A true leadership position in the family is to provide kids with an environment that says, "It's safe to try it, it's safe to fail. And if you fail, pick yourself up, learn from it, and go on." This is the same kind of environment that God provides for us as parents: we have the right to fail. As parents we're going to make mistakes, but God still loves us. He doesn't always like what we do, but He always loves us.

8

Walls
Are Not For People

Finding competent professional help can become a very difficult task. I can recall answering the phone and having a voice on the other end ask the question, "How much do you charge?"

I used to simply say $45.00 per session, and at that point the voice on the other end would say thank you and hang up. I've learned through these experiences to tell people who ask that question that I will be very happy to answer their question. But before I do, I say, "You know, there are several questions that you should be asking me other than how much money I charge." Some of those questions might be: What kind of a person are you? Are you married? Do you have a family? Do you value marriage? Do you have any spiritual values? What is your training? Is there a particular model you follow in your therapy with couples, individuals, or families?"

I realize that we live in a money-oriented society. It might seem wise to shop around for a bargain, but there is no such thing as a "good deal" in therapy. Essentially, you get what you pay for. Now please don't misunderstand this to mean that people who don't charge anything aren't worth anything. Nothing could be further from the truth. I've found that some pastors, priests, and people within the field of Christian education are very useful and productive resources. It doesn't always matter what kind of degree the person has behind his name, but what *does* matter is the particular skills he or she possesses. I personally believe that a good counselor is someone who knows when he's in over his head, and is willing to refer a client elsewhere or to consult with another professional.

Most experts realize that a great majority of counseling transpires within the confines of the church. This is indeed a viable place to seek refuge. Most people feel very comfortable with a pastor, priest, or rabbi, knowing that what they talk about is going to be held in the strictest confidence.

The great majority of people whom I see in my private work are directly referred to me by physicians, pastors, schoolteachers, and administrators. However, about 20 percent of my private work comes to me via the Yellow Pages. It's frightening to think that people find professionals with whom to share their most intimate thoughts through the Yellow Pages, but it does happen.

I feel committed to give the first-time client as much information as he or she feels necessary about myself as a person and as a therapist, in order to give him or her the opportunity to really look me over. It's important that the client feels comfortable with me. It's also important that we discuss at our first session the financial responsibilities of the client. Generally speaking, counselors and psychologists are willing to be paid on a monthly-payment basis. I've found that most clients realize that in any business, expenses are incurred and payments are necessary in order to keep the business going.

When seeking a professional person, above everything else *look for a therapist who is going to try to "get rid of you."* In other words, look for someone who is going to deal with you on as short a term as possible. Many counselors and psychologists feel that no behavioral change can take place without a long-term commitment— for example, one or two sessions per week for a year. I personally have not found this to be necessary in my private work. By not locking a client into long-term therapy, we're saying that we feel they can handle their responsibilities and decisions in the real world.

If in doubt, and if a physician or pastor isn't available to refer you to a professional, it might be wise to call the State Board of Psychologists Examiners, or a local psychological association, or the local chapter of the American Association of Marriage and Family Counselors. They could at least provide a list of people who are certified professionals. This in no way certifies that the therapist is right for you as the client, but it does protect you in the sense that all the people listed in the various associations have at least met minimum requirements. In some states, for example, a person can call himself a counselor without any training or any degree whatever. So it's important to know with whom you're going to be working. Don't be afraid to ask questions; you're paying good dollars to receive professional help, and you have every right to find out as much information as you need about the therapist.

Don't be misguided by selecting a counselor or psychologist solely on the basis that he or she is a Christian. Just because he is a Christian does not necessarily make him competent to help you. One of the basic decisions I made several years ago was not to designate my private practice as a Christian counseling service. I've been happy to this day that I didn't. The real joy of working in the "people business" comes from working with the non-Christian, the person who is spiritually oblivious to that side of life. Quite frankly, too many of us as Christians are hung up on the fact that God can't forgive us because the kinds of transgressions we have made in our lives are too great for God to forgive! I realize that many people choose Christian counselors and psychologists on the basis that they feel they will be better understood. I'm not putting down Christian counselors and psychologists; I'm merely saying that this should not be the only basis for selecting a counselor or psychologist.

It seems that so many people whom I see in my private work have had a very negative walk with God. Their up-bringing and training have been largely predicated on "don't do this" and "don't do that"—what I call *negative Christianity*, a Christianity that stresses the negative and does not stress the positive fact that God indeed has a purpose for our lives. Usually in working with a client, I get around to the eventual questions, "What are you really doing here in life?" "What is it all about?" "Do you feel there is a purpose to your being born?" I've found that most people are startled by these questions; they don't really know how to react. Most people say they want to be happy, but acknowledge the fact that they're not.

I think of Jackie, age 28, who came to me several months ago for individual therapy. At 28, she was still single and searching for reasons for her social isolation. One of the very first things I noticed about Jackie was the fact she did a very good job of hiding herself. She was really a very pretty woman who did a fantastic job of making herself appear very plain. Even in the spring heat of Arizona she wore long-sleeved sweaters and blouses.

Jackie made great progress in a very short period of time. One of her first assignments was to go home and categorize her entire wardrobe. She was amazed at her propensity to purchase baggy, long-sleeved sweaters and tops. Most of them fell in the category of the dark browns and greens as opposed to the light pastel colors. One of the things that meant so much to Jackie was a statement I made one evening: "Jackie, walls are not for people—they are for termites."

Jackie had successfully burrowed herself in the wall of life for a number of years. She had been afraid to come out to be noticed, out of a fear of being criticized or put down. But then Jackie began to make the necessary changes that were needed in her life. She shed her glasses for some contact lenses, and she got her hair cut and restyled in a most complimentary way. She also began to lose weight. I mention this because it was only by doing these things that Jackie convinced herself that she was indeed ready for behavioral change in her life. Her *action* reinforced her attitude. It was only a short time later that people began to notice the vast changes in Jackie. She saw that God could only use her as an effective witness in life if she would free herself from "the wall."

At one time Jackie described herself as a "wallflower" beginning as a young child and remaining so throughout her first 28 years. Jackie took refuge in the Scripture that states that God takes care of the birds of the field, so He's certainly going to take care of those who claim to be His own. It was only through courage and commitment to action that Jackie was able to turn her life around.

I remember telling Jackie that life was very much like a football game—that she was the quarterback in life going to the line of scrimmage and bending over the center, ready to take the snap of the ball. She had to look over the defense, and if the defense was such that it required "calling an audible" at the line of scrimmage, she had to do just that.

We compared this with the social situations in life that confront us every day. Jackie had to stop and ask herself the question in this social situation, "How would *old* Jackie react?" After answering that question to herself, she must proceed to call an "audible" at the line of scrimmage in order to change the play. It takes that kind of cognitive commitment and awareness to effect behavioral change in people. Once the commitment is made, people have to develop means to keep themselves going.

In Dr. Olson's book entitled *Can You Wait Till Friday?* he tells of a lone survivor of a boating accident who had apparently swum a great distance to shore. She had kept herself going by talking to herself and saying as she swam, "Just one more stroke." When they found her on the shore, she was semiconscious, still uttering the words, "Just one more stroke . . . just one more stroke . . . just one more stroke." Yes, beautiful cathedrals are built one brick at a time; a commitment has to start someplace. The cathedral and the shoreline might seem insurmountable if we fail to attack them with one action at a time.

According to all of her ex-boyfriends, Sally, age 22, tried too hard! She was always available, always willing to cook meals, always willing to do whatever they wanted. Much of her life seemed to say that she only counted in life if she pleased others. At age 22, she had all the makings of a super-martyr.

Sally was a beautiful, blue-eyed, blonde-haired girl, very trim and neat, with a vivacious personality. Sally told of the many times she had been used by men, beginning at age 16. Even her last sexual experience was as unfulfilling, unrewarding, and unsatisfying as her first one at age 16.

As we began to take a look at her life, I tried to show Sally that she had very little respect for herself and communicated this very readily to men, who were most willing to take advantage of her. It was only the grace of

God and the spiritual commitments which she had made that turned her life around.

After making these commitments in her life, Sally shared with me that her boyfriend had come over to her apartment ostensibly for sex. She told him very matter-of-factly that she wasn't interested. He left that night in a huff, but was back for several visits during the next few weeks and continued to be rebuffed. As the word got around throughout their social circles that Sally was no longer available for sex on a minute's notice, her circle of friends began to change drastically. She made the commitment that she was going to begin a regular program of worship and service.

Her life has been changing for the better ever since. Occasionally she still gets down on herself and expects a little too much, but she continues to grow and to enhance her self-image, and she commands the respect of young men. She was giggling with glee as she told me that the boy she was dating had taken over a month just to get up the nerve to give her a kiss! Sally relished the thought and savored the feeling that she was special, and that God had a plan for her life.

Sally is going to make it in life, not because of Kevin Leman, but because she made the necessary spiritual commitment in her life to say, "Okay, God, I'll go where you want me to go, I'll do what you want me to do. I'm yours—use me as you see fit." Sally keeps in touch; every once in a while I get a call from her in which she shares what's going on in her life. She's been thoughtful enough to share with me some of the opportunities she's had to share her new faith in God with the young women that she sees in her daily life, many of whom are similar to the "old Sally." How exciting it is to see a life change!

Jim Young, (now the head coach at Purdue University)

came to the University of Arizona as head football coach from the University of Michigan in 1973. Coach Young inherited a losing football program which had not had a winning season in six years. Like most football coaches, he made the necessary predictions that he was going to get things together football-wise at the University of Arizona.

Coach Young called a team meeting of all ballplayers and coaches for 4 P.M. on a Friday afternoon. At 4 P.M. he got up and closed the door to the meeting room, locking it behind him. Over half of the ballplayers and embarrassed coaches missed the opportunity to hear Coach Young's first remarks as head mentor of the University of Arizona football team. I believe at that very moment Coach Young began to pull the rug out, holding people accountable for their decision not to be on time. If they chose to talk in the hallway instead of being in the room at 4 P.M., they were going to miss the meeting.

Jim Young went on to turn a very mediocre football program into one of the most promising football programs in the country today. Coupled with the dynamic leadership of Dr. John Schaefer, the young President of the University of Arizona, Coach Young's record served as the impetus for the University's affiliating with the prestigious PAC-10 conference. Coach Young went on to post a 31-13 record during his four-year tenure as head football coach!

Ballplayers and staff alike respected him because they always knew where they stood with him. The guidelines were there, and there were very few gray areas. We as parents can learn a lot from Coach Young. If we say something is going to happen, it had better happen. Guidelines need to be explicit, and the consequences for failure to follow guidelines need to be implemented. We need to be closing doors and locking them behind us in our daily walk with our children.

I have chosen to summarize some of the themes and ideas expressed in earlier chapters through guidelines I've entitled, "A Child's Ten Commandments to Parents." No doubt my list could be expanded to include as many as 20 or 30 items, but these particular 10 commandments seem to say it for me.

A CHILD'S TEN COMMANDMENTS TO PARENTS

1. My hands are small; please don't expect perfection whenever I make a bed, draw a picture, or throw a ball. My legs are short; please slow down so that I can keep up with you.
2. My eyes have not seen the world as yours have; please let me explore safely: don't restrict me unnecessarily.
3. Housework will always be there. I'm only little for such a short time—please take time to explain things to me about this wonderful world, and do so willingly.
4. My feelings are tender; please be sensitive to my needs; don't nag me all day long. (You wouldn't want to be nagged for your inquisitiveness.) Treat me as you would like to be treated.
5. I am a special gift from God; please treasure me as God intended you to do, holding me accountable for my actions, giving me guidelines to live by, and disciplining me in a loving manner.
6. I need your encouragement, but not your praise, to grow. Please go easy on the criticism; remember, you can criticize *the things I do* without criticizing *me*.
7. Please give me the freedom to make decisions concerning myself. Permit me to fail, so that I can learn from my mistakes. Then someday I'll be prepared to make the kind of decisions life requires of me.

8. Please don't do things over for me. Somehow that makes me feel that my efforts didn't quite measure up to your expectations. I know it's hard, but please don't try to compare me with my brother or my sister.

9. Please don't be afraid to leave for a weekend together. Kids need vacations from parents, just as parents need vacations from kids. Besides, it's a great way to show us kids that your marriage is very special.

10. Please take me to Sunday school and church regularly, setting a good example for me to follow. I enjoy learning more about God.

SELECTED REFERENCES

Christensen, Oscar. *Understanding of the Needs of Today's Youth.* Department of Counseling and Guidance, University of Arizona, 1970.

Dinkmeyer, Don, and McKay, Gary. *Raising a Responsible Child: Practical Steps to Successful Family Relationships.* New York: Simon and Schuster, 1973.

Dobson, James. *Dare to Discipline.* Wheaton, Ill.: Tyndale House Publishers, 1970; Glendale, Ca.: Regal Books, G/L Publications, 1970 (Co-published).

Dreikurs, R. *The Challenge of Parenthood.* New York: Hawthorne Press, 1948.

Dreikurs, R. and Grey L. *A Parent's Guide to Child Discipline.* New York: Hawthorne Press, 1970.

Dreikurs, R., and Soltz, V. *Children: The Challenge.* New York: Hawthorne Press, 1964.

Ginott, Haim G. *Between Parent and Teenager.* New York: Avon Books, 1969.

Hendricks, Howard. *Heaven Help the Home.* Wheaton, Ill.: Victor Books, SP Publications, 1973.

Leman, Kevin. *Children: Delight or Dilemma?* (cassette album). Phoenix, Ariz.: General Cassette Corporation, 1977.

Olson, Kenneth. *Can You Wait Till Friday?* Greenwich, CN: Fawcett Publication Books, 1975.

Powell, John. *The Secret of Staying in Love.* Niles, IL: Argus Communications, 1974.

Notes

Notes

Notes